Spirit, Word, and Story

Other Books by Calvin Miller

Apples, Snakes and Bellyaches
The Empowered Communicator
The Empowered Leader
A Hunger for Meaning
Marketplace Preaching
Once upon a Tree
Requiem for Love
The Singer Trilogy
Symphony in Sand series
The Table of Inwardness
Walking with the Angels

Spirit, Word, and Story

A Philosophy
of Marketplace Preaching

CALVIN MILLER

Baker Books

A Division of Baker Book House Co
Grand Rapids, Michigan 49516

© 1989, 1996 by Calvin Miller

Published by Baker Books
a division of Baker Book House Company
P.O. Box 6287, Grand Rapids, MI 49516-6287

First published in 1989 by Word Publishing as *Spirit, Word, and Story: A Philosophy of Preaching*

Printed in the United States of America

Library of Congress Cataloging-in-Publication Data
Miller, Calvin.
    Spirit, word, and story : a philosophy of marketplace preaching / Calvin Miller.
       p.   cm.
    Originally published : Dallas : Word Pub., c1989.
    Includes bibliographical references.
    ISBN 0-8010-9026-1 (pbk.)
    1. Preaching. I. Title.
    [BV4211.2.M49 1996]
    251—dc20   96-20274

Contents

Preface

Years ago I made up my mind to preach the Bible rather than to try to figure it out. I still want to dispense the various insights I have gleaned from my reading of Scripture, but I now design my sermons to redeem, not merely inform. All life needs redeeming—the lost from judgment, the saved from despair, disillusion, or religious boredom. Thus Christ is the redeeming need of those who have not found him and the redeeming need of those who *have*. If they are already in Christ, I want my sermons to move them even deeper into that most primary of all relationships.

After thirty years of preaching, I have never lost interest in the subject. I certainly want to do all I can to ensure that my listeners never lose interest in that subject either. So I am forever reading, listening, and attending seminars to improve my edge in preaching.

Why do both preachers and listeners have an intense interest in this subject? The sermon, for two thousand years now, has been the agony and ecstasy of all who bear it as a calling. Paul referred to the art of sermonizing as "the foolishness of preaching" (1 Cor. 1:21). Why refer to preaching this way? Paul knew the tension between the importance of preaching and the low esteem the world gave it.

At the outset of this study, let me say that I am aware that many books have been written on the subject. Homiletic texts, like diet books, proliferate, and both, I think, feed on a kind of neurosis. Often during the writing of this book, I asked myself, "Is it really necessary to have another book on the subject?" Still, here it is: preaching, the subject that both intrigues and embarrasses our world. Why? I believe we need books like this one because we all want to get better at what the world labels "foolishness." Small wonder we preachers are a mixture of ego and self-denial. We must preach the "humility of the cross" while all the time standing center stage, calling, instructing, and confronting.

At the preaching moment, our sermons are more than the sum of our earnestness and preparation. On a "good" Sunday, when the compliments are long (perhaps because the sermon is short), it is clear that our preaching is God's heritage and that we are the merchants of glory! Such pulpit stardom, however, fades fast on a hot July Sunday when hell or heaven seem weak concerns to a sun-worshiping flock, lollygagging at the lake. Then our preaching does seem foolish to us, and we fret as martyrs to our misery.

I have written this book out of that worldview which I believe to be most important. I am an evangelical pastor. For the thirty-five years of my ministry, I have tried to keep my preaching central, but low key.

I don't like designating myself with a category that sounds wishy-washy, but I am a middle-of-the-roader in most things. I have often, tongue-in-cheek, described myself as feeling comfortable with worship that is midway between Billy Sunday and the archbishop of Canterbury. The usual rejoinder to one claiming to be a middle-of-the-roader is that in the middle of the road, one gets shot at from both sides. I realize that this book will be read by those whose approach to worship may be more or less formal than my own. So if you are to my right, forgive my leftness; if to my left, forgive my rightness, and blessed be all who walk somewhere between the Latin Mass and youth camp devotionals.

The words that best describe both my preaching and worship might be *relational* and *casual*. Many rapidly growing churches would emphasize these same ideas. Nevertheless, a relational worship style does not mean that one can skimp at sermon preparation, nor assume that relational worship can ooze into easy togeth-erness without the discipline of well-planned worship and (above all) well-planned sermons.

I bring up my worship preference (and sermon style) to make it clear that all preaching must work within a framework of individu-ality. My particular emphasis on preaching cannot be yours—the world would find one of us unnecessary if we were exactly alike. My hope is that the principles of this text, however, will find us in agree-ment: Preaching is important, and the best components of our art remain unchanged from church to church.

Here is my own argument for the importance of preaching: Our unique lives and callings should emphasize the same biblical truths. If they do, our sermons, done differently, will speak of faith, and faith will make us one in purpose. After all, we have no need to be alike, but our truth *is* one and our sermons, artful or less so, should spend themselves in the telling of that truth.

Introduction

R. E. C. Browne wrote, "Religion is not a way of mastering . . . complexity, but of bearing it."[1] This is true also of sermons. Life for all of us has a way of being complex and ponderous. The sermon cannot eliminate life's complexity, but it should bear up under that complexity, pointing, at least, to a healing simplicity. No sermon can answer every heartache, but every sermon should be an existential cry of hope.

I have always been reluctant to claim that my preaching is merely simplifying the human dilemma with "rosy" sermons, but I know that without continually preaching the ideal life, human existence can clot in miring, fatiguing disillusionment. Like Francis of Assisi, the servant sermon should come down from its dais of glory to embrace lepers with this consolation: "You shall not bear this alone!" Preaching, then, is glory made wise with compassion.

No book on any subject tells all the truth about that subject. G. K. Chesterton observed, "Anyone writing so small a book about so big a man must leave out something."[2] Needless to say, anyone daring to write a book about so vast a subject as the sermon must, of necessity, leave something out, and so, no doubt, will I. Why this incomplete volume, then?

I have set my reason for writing in the title: *Spirit, Word, and Story.* As the triptych suggests, I will deal first with the Spirit's place in preaching. Next I will look at preaching's relationship to God's Word and how it relates to all words as the building blocks of communication. Finally, I will deal with story—the use of illustration, parable, and the development of a narrative style.

The final part of the book looks at the preparation and delivery of sermons as the discipline of pulpit communication. I don't present my insights as "how-to's." There are many fine preaching texts available that deal with more mechanical matters; this book is intended to be a philosophy of preaching.[3] As such, I shall present broad suggestions by which any preacher might arrive at an effective style of preparation and delivery. Like fingerprints, our own unique style individualizes our sermons. My concern for this book, then, is to serve both those who may preach propositionally oriented sermons and those who may be more story-oriented in their gospel presentation. I do this, however, with a clear bias: The gospel is primarily a story event. We are saved by the story and our faith in it. The precepts by which we express our faith come later.

Let me state at the outset a strong conviction: It is most important to work at a style of sermonizing that fits your personality. Many effective psychological inventories are available to help each of us discover what we are really like. If on the Myers-Briggs, for example, your category indicates a "thinking" personality, which may have strong propensity for precept preaching, then your sermon style might vary vastly from those with more "feeling" styles of personality, who would preach in more emotive modes.

It is oversimplifying to say that some of us are right-brain dominated, with a flair for the narrative, and others are left-brain dominated, with more strengths in precept. Still, those more influenced by the left brain will be drawn to precept preaching; those more influenced by the right brain will be likely to preach story sermons. Story preachers tend to rail on precept preachers as wooden expositors, and precept preachers tend to look down on story preachers as fluffy or frothy.

I hope to make it difficult in this book for anyone to use the right-brain or left-brain personality style as an excuse for not developing as broad a pulpit presentation as possible. Most people live in an arena of thinking that balances right- and left-brain techniques. Precept and story always make the best impact when they are used together in the sermon.

Can Great Preaching Be Taught?

I once knew a woman whose job it was to secure student preachers through a seminary. After listening to the sermons of these fledglings, she called the seminary placement officer and said, "Why can't you send us a young preacher who can preach?" The placement officer replied, "We can't make preachers out of people who don't have any 'preach' in them!" Giving natural talent its due, that statement is false. This book presupposes that preaching *can* be taught.

All preachers have their own natural hints of expression. Passion, for example, is a key ingredient in preaching and exists more naturally in some than others. The love of books, by which sermons grow wise and helpful, is found more readily in some. Personal drive, empathy, and spiritual discipline are qualities found in varying amounts among preachers. Whatever our natural gifts, they can all be developed to maximize the impact of the sermon.

Let's examine the facets of inspired preaching by beginning at the point of spiritual discipline. The one quality that congregations are most reluctant to forgive in a pastor is a lack of acquaintance with God. Spiritual discipline is the hard work of sermon preparation. To be effective, this kind of discipline needs to be both voluntary and consistent. No Christian can mature without it. How, then, shall a preacher preach without it? Pastors must be possessed of a radiant spiritual discipline that keeps them studying the Scripture. Their personal pietism must keep in touch with that power that infuses sermons with meaning and hope.

There is an old cliché made popular by traveling evangelists: "The reason that most churches can't be revived is that they have never been 'vived' in the first place." Remember also Wesley's lament on the way back from his disappointing American missionary experience: "I went to America to convert the Indians, but who shall convert me?"

Precept preachers are, by their very nature, more given to consistent spiritual disciplines (and for that matter, discipline of any sort) than story-oriented preachers. Story-oriented preachers need to beware of the ease with which they lapse into the emotive and relational channels of preaching. They often tend to "relate" their way through the sermon, leaving out tough discipline. They trust that their post-sermonic glad-handing and what Father Divine used to call "tangibilitation" will grant them forgiveness for an impoverished piety and thin study. They glitter so easily in a group that they often depend entirely on their relational skills to get them through all of life. Precept preachers are not necessarily introverts, but they do operate in life as they preach—with outlines of one sort or another. They tend to schedule everything they do as if each item were a sermon outline.

It is not proper to set passion and instruction across from each other, because good preaching contains both. The opposite of passion is deadness, but it may appear to be instruction. One might ask how passion and instruction differ. Passion likes to tell stories that inflame, amuse, or bring tears. Instruction seems to switch off passion as easily as it switches on the overhead projector. The passionate preacher is more interested in the artfulness of the message, while the precept preacher gets more excited about truth than the way it is told. In this book, we will work to avoid the either/or of story versus precept. Those prone to tell stories and string them together in a pointless, if interesting, way need to work at outlining and linking their stories with reason and precept. Precept preachers, on the other hand, can with a little practice learn the art of illustrating. Remember, precept may teach, but story fascinates. Story keeps the attention of the listener as the teacher transfers great propositions from the speaker's mind to the listener's mind.

Whatever our natural bent, all of us are under obligation to refine our craft. Real learning demands change, and implicit in all change is effort. Each time I have set out to correct a deficiency in my sermon preparation or delivery, I have found that I had to work much harder than I wanted to in correcting that deficiency. For example, I had to rid my speech of what Edwin Newman called the "y'know" syndrome. This affectation consists of making "y'know" a vocalized pause that nervously fills in the silences of oratory with a distraction. I corrected this habit only through utter concentration. I also decided very late in my career to extemporize my sermons and no longer read from a manuscript. Speaking extempore was frightening and difficult to master once the security of my heavy manuscript was gone. When that fear was remedied, I decided to remove the pulpit. Without the constriction of a pulpit, my preaching took on a more intimate quality. After twenty-two years of standing behind a pulpit, I felt insecure at first as I preached in the wide open. Having nothing to fix me geographically to the chancel, I resorted to a nervous pacing. Only with the greatest concentration was I able to control this distracting nervousness. Eliminating each of these petty habits enabled me to improve gradually the quality of my communication.

The Sermon and the Altar

In every church the sermon is delivered from or near the altar area. Even in its pre-Reformation origins, the sermon was intimately bound to the mass, and the mass was set at the altar. The sermon has always been seen as a deeply serious communication issuing from the depths of the sacrifice of Christ. After the Reformation, the Brethren movement, Baptists, and Methodists viewed the altar as a place of decision for Christ. These decisions might be first-time surrenders to the gospel, confessions of backsliding, or times of getting right with God. In general, these decisions were motivated by the high exhortation of the sermon. While not all sermons today end with decision times, let's consider the importance of the altar.

Since my own tradition incorporates an open altar in worship, I have come to believe that the sermon is servant to what some theologians in other contexts have called the "demand" of God. Older evangelists in the Baptist church talked about "preaching for decisions." This means that the sermon is to exhort the listeners to declare publicly the conclusion that they have reached in their hearts during the preaching of the sermon. This is particularly so when those conclusions have had life-changing impact.

Sermons that seek to motivate listeners to move to the altar lose much of their *art qua art* form. Therefore, Episcopal preachers are more likely to see the sermon as art than those in the Pentecostal tradition. An empty altar following a sermon in a highly evangelistic church is often taken as a sign that God is not moving at all in the church. In such a strict view, however, the sermon comes to be seen as salesmanship and the altar response as the close of the sale. I am not so severe in grading my own sermons. I learned long ago that if I am to have peace in Christ, I must not link my sermons too closely to the altar response. Most preachers who have this severe view of the altar inevitably live in guilt when few people come forward.

Christianity's inherent heart of conversion is at once its greatest strength and a glaring weakness. I list it as a weakness because our desire to see people saved can result in a neurotic preoccupation with counting decisions and even competing from church to church for numerical response. We have frequently claimed that witnessing is "sharing the gospel in the power of the Spirit and leaving the results to God." If our burden over empty altars steals our sense of peace, it is clear that we have not learned to leave the obligation of response where it belongs—with the worshiper!

Is the altar that important in churches that do not have public decision times? Even though the altar in the public-decision church may tell the herald how effectively he has spoken, the sermon in any church must still be a form of dialogue between the speaker and the listeners. The audience should remain in a decision mode as they reckon with the herald and wrangle inwardly with the sermon's logic. Ideally, they should be motivated to decide something, at least in their hearts. They must kneel at the inward altar that is suggested by the outer altar. If they do not approach

16

that inward altar, the sermon cannot have succeeded. Saint Teresa of Avila suggested that the real Christ is the Christ of a few centimeters who rules from the tiny, heart-sized throne in the center of our lives.

Leo Tolstoy describes the event of his conversion in the highly autobiographical *Memoirs of a Lunatic*. Tolstoy found himself receiving new life in Christ at a communion service. With no public declaration, his heart found high adoration and then decision. John Wesley had the same experience at Aldersgate in a more public way, and started the movement that was ultimately characterized by open decisions.

The Sermon Is Not a Speech

What does the altar really say about the nature of the sermon? I believe it says four things. First, the sermon is no more a mere speech than the Bible is a mere book. The sermon may involve the use of the same communication skills that a speech might use, but at its heart the sermon exists on a deeper, more existential level than a speech. The very character of a sermon says, "What I am saying has more eternal implications than a speech and will make the highest possible demand upon your life." Further, the sermon trumpets, "I am speaking with an authority beyond myself and dealing with values born in another realm. I am not preaching this primarily as an art form or as a partisan platform. Just as the word 'fire' in a crowded theater is not to be admired and heeded because it is artfully declared, so my words are not designed to have you praise the oratory, but to alert you to particular needs."

The altar is not Hyde Park. It is not a Dale Carnegie lecture hall. It is not Toastmasters. The very architecture of the altar says to the listeners, "Notice the colored glass, the cross, the organ pipes, the austere pulpit, the hangings!" All of these special effects say, "This is the place where God speaks, and my words contain his words! Stand, then, and hear the word of the Lord!"

The Altar Presupposes the Gift of Time

Churches will seldom grow hardy on fifty-five-minute worship services. In any atmosphere where getting through on time is more important than content, the power of the sermon is lost. I have always believed that sermons should be short, and have long argued that the heart cannot absorb more than the seat can endure. But it is difficult for people to come out of the secular world and be challenged by thirty minutes of song and fifteen minutes of sermon and then make life-changing decisions.

I am no longer concerned with 11:55 dismissals. I now give warm worship and developmental logic the time they need to produce change. "Sermonettes" do, in a sense, produce "Christianettes." Real altars are agonizing places of change, and lasting change derives from adequate confrontation. Altars require the time necessary to reckon with our needs and answer them.

The Altar Is a Forum for Existence Rather Than Education

This may be crudely stated, but it bears firm truth: Altars have to do with *being* rather than *learning*. Perhaps this was one of the great differences between the synagogue of classic Judaism and the church as Christ (and later Paul) spoke of it. Synagogues were primarily places of learning, like schools. The church, however, has ever been the assembly of saints meeting to encounter God. Learning should occur in a sermon, for nobody admires a naive Christian, but the altar is a place of encounter that develops *being*. While the church may be there to teach and educate in the Scriptures, the altar is the place where daring and dialogue meet.

In essence, all being reaches for relationship, either to gain it for the first time or to strengthen and define it. It is here that the precept preacher must take note: The church does exist as a center for Bible education, but if congregants come and gather and then go without encounter, the church has failed to understand the sermon's highest calling—change!

18

The words *didache* and *kerygma* define somewhat the milieu of preaching. In post–New Testament times *didache* was a word that defined the teaching function of the church. The word *kerygma* had more to do with exhortation and appeal. The *didache* was given, of course, to enrich understanding of the Scriptures, but *kerygma* was the inescapable altar demand: "You must know God! And if you know him already, you must know him better!"

The Altar Is the Place of Mystery

One cannot attend a mass without being struck by the mystery of the inscrutable God. This was particularly true in the first fifteen centuries of the Roman church. Protestants, however, have demythologized the church, sometimes to the point that they have left the altar too low and worship too plain.

My suspicion is that God is more apt to change those who live in awe of him than those who have merely recorded his attributes in their sermon notebooks. The story-oriented sermon is less adamant in its confrontation. The precept sermon nails down more vital truths but tends to strut the triumphalism of its flawless study.

The preacher who uses stories to say, "This is how we are like God or in need of God," gives the impression, as Michael Polanyi says, that "we know more than we can tell."[4] We do, indeed, know more than we tell, for we are primarily experiencers of a grace that nobody in the world can explain. But story preaching says to the listener, "Pay attention: Our truth is larger than our sermons."

Eugene Lowry favors sermon stories to keep a sense of the greatness and awe of God. "Once a proposition is stated," says Lowry, "it is done; closure has occurred, and only with great difficulty can one get things moving again."[5] How true! Stories carry the listener along, but precepts tend to say the trip is over. Stories speak to the mystery we feel when we think of God. Precepts say, "Well, folks, this is a great truth; write it down, and I'll see you at the cafeteria as soon as I get out of these vestments."

For this reason, so many homileticians advise us to start our sermons with a story. It is not only the best way to interest our listeners in our sermon, but it keeps blatant precepts from closing down the mind at the start of things. Story and the altar should combine to hold interest by spinning images that snare us in the life-changing encounter. Image is the bait that keeps us snapping at the golden precepts of dogma.

Sermon Preparation

All of the ideas that I have introduced so far will, of course, comprise the substance of this book. At the end of the book are two chapters that deal with the specific aspects of preparation and delivery not otherwise covered in the main corpus of this text, but before we complete this introduction, let us briefly look at the text and context of sermon preparation.

Text

The Bible is, of course, the textbook for our lives and preachment. There is no substitute for a profound respect and use of this Book. The immensity of its truth is wide enough to speak to every real need of life. I have heard of preachers who claim to have exhausted its wisdom and then have put it aside to preach the Bhagavad-Gita or the works of William Shakespeare. Such preaching is not only wrong, it ceases to be Christian. To see the Scriptures as divinely inspired means that God is working on both ends of scriptural inspiration. On the writer's end of the Bible, God inspires the text as adequate to human need. On the listener's end, God quickens the text in proclamation to effect inner change. I cannot countenance any sermon which proceeds from any other base than holy text.

Context

This means that neither the Bible writers nor we who preach their words can separate God's Word from our words, nor his life from ours. Each of us does not merely live, we move through life. We are spending our years to purchase wisdom. We, like those who care nothing for our preachment, are social beings. We all must live and die in communion with the secular world. This world contains truths other than those we champion in the pulpit. The preacher who integrates the most worthy secular truths into his sermons adds richness to his preaching.

The secular world can intimidate us, however, and keep us running back to our cloistered sermon world to feel secure in our protected religious system. But every time we step outside our pulpit world, there again we encounter our secular milieu with all its challenges to spiritual values.

Preachers must live in the secular world, yet not accept its bogus or immoral values, lest after we have gained a hearing, we have nothing to say. Once we walk with certainty in our entire world, the sermon can throb with a courage it did not learn by hiding out in warm religious ghettos. This does not mean that we bring the entire world into the pulpit, but that we realize that hard-hitting preachers are not monks practicing closed truths in religious closets.

I, for instance, know that Shakespeare was not an evangelical with strong convictions on heaven and hell. He did, however, touch on large themes of life and relationship. He thus finds his way into many of my sermons. My love for the Bard is part of my life context and value system. By contrast, one of my Omaha pastor friends is a sports fan. He can name all the players on the Dodgers as easily as I can name all the Montagues or Capulets! Hence, his messages are more athletic, less literary than mine and often contain references, illustrations, and allusions from the world of sports.

The point is, we all must live in a wider world than the world of the church. I like to think of this wider world as our "preaching habitat." Whatever we enjoy—from athletics to the theater, from the funny papers to the theological journals—is our life context. When the preacher welds his secular interests to the Bible, preaching becomes intriguing and powerful! The preaching habitat gives the sermon soul and human interest. The biblical text makes the sermon powerful and confrontational. All great preaching, I think, that survives well in a local church situation successfully sets the preaching text within the life context.

We are ready to proceed with our discussion of the various components of the preparation and delivery of sermons. It is not important that we agree everywhere, nor that our views of preaching be brought to a common mind, but it is my hope that this book will provide for us a common ground for entering into dialogue. This book, like the sermon itself, will fail if you and I do not meet and react to each other. If that happens, we shall both widen our minds and extend his kingdom. What a great double goal for our lives!

Part 1

Spirit

1

The Imperative Mystery of Preaching

The nature of true, pure contemplation is such that, while kindling the heart with divine love, it sometimes fills it with great zeal to win other souls for God. The heart gladly gives up the quiet of contemplation for the work of preaching. Once its desires are fulfilled, the heart quickly returns to contemplation, as to the source of good works.

Bernard of Clairvaux

All we taste, against all we lack, is like a single drop of water against the whole sea, for we feed upon His Immensity, which we cannot devour, and we yearn after His Infinity, which we cannot attain.

John Ruysbroeck

Bishops still wear headgear ("mitres") shaped like cloven tongues of flame to symbolize how the church was born.

Harry Blamires

We who preach are indebted to the ancient Romans for the name of our art. *Sermon* is a Latin word (*sermo, sermonis*) that Cicero and others applied to their orations. It meant "speech" to them, and they were satisfied to see it that way. The church borrowed their word and baptized it with a definition worthy of its calling.

How is a sermon different from a speech? Well, some would quickly point out (with redundance) that a sermon is "preachier" than a speech. Others point out that it is uncommonly longer. Psychologists might say that it is more guilt producing, biased, coercive, or opinionated.

The sermon is a speech that is otherworldly. Before you close this book thinking that it is not going to be a book on preaching that touches the world at hand, let us remember that all great preaching is otherworldly. The sermon's otherworldliness is the sermon's intrigue, its mystery.

The preacher stands between two worlds and speaks. If he takes either of these worlds lightly, then, of course, he is not preaching in the most effective manner. If he takes the world at hand lightly, then his sermons will be unusable and of little interest to the hassled, contemporary parishioner. If he takes too lightly the world of the Spirit, then he will not have furnished his listeners with the real firepower required in handling life in the now.

One often hears the complaint, "Some people in the church are so heavenly minded they are of no earthly good!" Here I add a word of protest. Very few people (if any) have ever really fit that description. The truth is, those who have preached in such a way as to change this world have been "heavenly minded" and have thus been of much earthly good. Consider the real picture a moment. Jesus, our Redeemer, came from outside this world saying things like, "I am the living bread that came down from heaven" (John 6:51), "My kingdom is not of this world" (John 18:36), and, "As it is, you do not belong to the world" (John 15:19).

Then as he neared his ascension, he said, "It is for your good that I am going away. Unless I go away, the Counselor will not come" (John 16:7). As he ascended, two men in white said very frankly to the agog pedestrians watching the launch, "Men of Galilee, why do you stand looking into the sky? This Jesus, who has been taken up from you into heaven, will come in just the same way as you have watched

Him go into heaven" (Acts 1:11 NASB). Since that moment, Jesus has been elsewhere in the cosmos (at least away from the planet), and hence, otherworldly.

Further, any number of passages teach that we are headed for where he is, and there in the sweet (otherworldly) by and by we will reckon with our failures, be crowned, and so on. While we don't sing as often as our forebears did about this other world, reminiscences nonetheless still come through our worship, and the point is established—our destiny and preachment are bound to another world. Our whole calling is beside the point if our sermons cease to address this world.

The primary burden of the preacher lies in making the more distant world real. William Wordsworth, standing upon a city bridge, surmised (maybe sermonized), "The world is too much with us / Late and soon, getting and spending / We lay waste our powers."[1] How can we who are so bound to this nearer world raise much interest in the world of the spirit? Yogi Berra is credited with having said, "You can see a lot by observing."[2] Looking around is the key to growth and understanding in every field, but in preaching the *sine qua non* is that the sermon must make visible the unseeable realm.

The sermon that succeeds in this task inundates the crowd in mystery. Seeing the unseeable rouses this imperative mystery. What we can see may be interesting, but not for long; the things which are clear are soon only curios about which we are not curious. God's revelation of himself is real but somehow shadowy. We only pry at it, having enough of it to convince ourselves that there is a God, but not enough to have all that we want of God. The sermon which makes real the hiddenness of God holds compelling interest. Oddly, to make God's hiddenness real has very little to do with the sermon in either its preparation or delivery. The preacher's own pilgrimage and hunger for this elusive God is what creates an alluring mystery in sermons.

The Intrigue of Otherworldliness

We are always more interested in what we don't have than what we do have. Materialism, therefore, cannot enthrall. Grasping after the intangible is the earnest pursuit of real interest. When the Holy Spirit invades our sermons, the other world looms almost visible as the flock is inflamed with intrigue. Let us consider the otherworldliness of the sermons in the Bible. Jesus' preaching had an otherworldly tone. In the Sermon on the Mount, he mentions heaven (or "the kingdom of" or "our Father in") some dozen times. He mentions hell and ever-lasting destruction a half-dozen times. In speaking of heaven and hell, he uses parables of roads, last judgments, and moral lifestyles.

John the Baptist (in Luke 3 and John 1) appears as a fiery preacher speaking of the coming kingdom and the apocalyptic wrath of God. Peter's Whitsunday sermon is an account of the invasion of this world by the Holy Spirit (taken from Joel 2) and a clear statement that Jesus had been raised from the dead and had taken his place at the right hand of the Father (Acts 2:32–33). Stephen's sermon, which ended in his martyrdom, quotes Isaiah 66:1–2, "Heaven is my throne, and the earth is my footstool." At the end of the sermon Stephen says that he sees "heaven open" and Jesus standing at the right hand of God (Acts 7:56). Paul, in his sermon on Mars Hill, makes it clear that the God of Christianity is transcendent: "The God who made the world and everything in it is the Lord of heaven and earth and does not live in temples built by hands" (Acts 17:24).

From first to last, otherworldliness is what brings to the pulpit such interest as it has. Great preachers of every generation have been oth-erworldly in their sermons. As preachers become removed from that pursuit, interest in the pulpit declines.

The word *sermon* implies the presence of God in the words of what otherwise would be only a speech. Without the Holy Spirit and his creative and recreative activity there can be words, or essays, or the reading of papers, but there can be no preaching.[3] When the Spirit comes into our speaking, our words are no longer a speech. They are a sermon, and they possess the capacity for authentic spiritual encounter.

Here intrigue is born. People do not attend churches that answer their questions. They attend churches that create mystery. When potential members visit a church, they come again only if that church is in touch with the world they hunger for, not the one where they live. We too long have seen the preacher as a kind of this-world guru with a pocket full of answers. Churches that operate by this role model are churches that may expect to decline. First of all, there are too many questions, and once any question is answered, the preacher is driven back to the study to dredge up more answers. But more important than whether the preacher *can* answer questions is whether the preacher *ought* to. The answered question only files the issue in "finished" business. The unanswerable question is always a vital subject for intrigue.

Mystery answers not questions, but life! Give me the mystery, for only when people see their many needs as being solved in the mystery does the church become important to them. Most people are willing to bear the burdens that the church cannot lift if they are made to understand that beyond this world is a God who cares and lifts the heavy parts of life with promises of deliverance. Jesus is the earnest bearer of the promise. Life was harsh to Christ, even as it is to most, but he died as a lesson that not all of life's problems are solvable in this world. In fact, the great injustices make no sense and are completely solvable only in the world that is on the way.

The preacher is not a guru; he is a reminder that life can have meaning when seen from the proper vantage point. The preacher's words from week to week ought to be an audible reminder that the Spirit of Power can invade the world that doesn't matter with the one that does. Furthermore, when the preacher's faith is as radiant as it needs to be—with God's very presence—he is a role model for trusting.

I am not suggesting that the preacher has to be perfect all the time. No congregation is composed of dolts; they understand that the herald's humanity is as real as their own. I am only saying that if the struggle of faith and the reality of faith are not obvious in the preacher's life, then the possibility for real ministry is missing. More importantly, the imperative mystery that binds a congregation in this liminal togetherness will also be missing.

Perhaps *liminal* is the real word here. Theodore Roszak has reminded us that the best role model for a preacher is that of a shaman. Forgive the pagan insinuation, but a shaman in his primitive culture is the one whose life cannot be understood rationally. I am setting the word *liminal* across from the word *logical*. The liminal figure is one whose life cannot be described by reason. The shaman's life (as viewed by his tribe) is one through which strange forces are at play. His whole bearing is one of intrigue. Roszak and others warn that we must not let this otherworldly mystique be so hungered for that the congregation champions religious psychotics, but it is also very clear that logic and "this-world" rhetoric have never been nor ever will be at the center of the Christian faith.

Sermons are the documents of all that cannot be documented— namely, mystery. Mystery is fearsome to the touch—the knowable, the unknown, the light we see through a glass darkly (1 Cor. 13:12). We who preach are blind heralds who trust but do not understand our heraldry.

The sermon will have no greater friend than the spiritual dependency of the pastor. If the preacher really needs God, his search and hunger will inflame his little words. The mystery of the Spirit will gild human syllables till they glitter with the presence of God.

The devotional life of the pastor is so important because his devotional life puts him in touch with the world of the Spirit, and that world supplies the vitality of his preaching. A devotional spirit cannot hide itself. No matter how the pastor tries, the most obvious thing about him, to those who attend his sermons, will be his touch, or lack of touch, with God. This is not to say that sermons cannot be well written and preached from a strictly oratorical basis. Of course they can. They may even be well attended, but the dimensions of real change come from a life of devotion.

When the Scriptures have been taught as best we can, and the moral reinforcers have been heralded as best we can, *we* are still not the substance of a sermon. Orthodoxy can be preached regularly and never live. Commandments and covenants can be repeated until both preacher and congregation are dull of hearing. But the pastor in touch with God is a fire that spawns intrigue, and miracles, it would seem, spring up around such faith. There is little wonder that Charles Finney said, "We have had instruction until we are hardened. It is time for us to pray!"[4]

30

While I want to be firm in this matter of the pastor's devotional life, I also want to sound a warning. The pastor must not adopt a messiah complex and think that the spiritual life of everyone in the church is the result of his own. Feeling the responsibility for others' shortcomings only creates neuroses. The preacher who assumes, "If only I were more regular in prayer, the commitment of my people would deepen," is setting himself up for a great fall. Even Jesus never assumed responsibility for someone else's inwardness or lack of it. Christ only preached the inner kingdom, leaving the construction of that kingdom up to those who attended his sermons.

When the pastor's life is bound devotionally to Christ, the sermon will not be as fixed as homileticians might like. The sermon may even lose some of its literary character. Perhaps you are asking yourself, "Is that any way for a man who's writing a book on preaching to talk?" It is time to state the thesis of my life and, I hope, this book: I would like for us to see that preaching fine sermons is not an end in God's kingdom. Preaching is a tool—one of remonstrance, instruction, and change. The qualities to which the sermon aims are best not set in oratory. They're best set in life, searching, spontaneity, and prayer. This is the liminal aspect of our calling. When we have thoroughly prepared our sermons (and we should), and when we have used the best tools of exegesis (and we should), then comes the waiting aspect of the sermon that immerses it in a synergism beyond itself. Sermons fall short of all biblical models when they are only the best of study, preparation, and delivery.

What exactly does the Spirit do to make the speech a sermon? Donald Coggan says that he stimulates, even awakens, but the strength of his work is to animate what would otherwise be merely dead words: "The French word *animateur* gets close to an element which, in the context of preaching, is highly significant. For it suggests that, as the preacher does his preparation or takes his stand in the pulpit, he is not alone. Beside him, within him, is the Stimulator-Spirit, the Lord, the Life-Giver, ready to enliven."[5] The Spirit as animator is the power source, the evidence that the Almighty has invaded our words to get his work done.

31

The preacher who sets the crown of intrigue upon the predictable worship service must always be careful that he honors two things. First, he must honor the sacredness of all personalities. It is no secret that our ability to love others is clearly rooted in our own self-acceptance. If we live with an incessant spirit of self-deprecation, we will likewise preach a harsh gospel. We may only make God our flamethrower to debilitate those whose spirituality seems substandard by our devoted evaluation. To deal with their poor commitment, we may "tack their hides to the wall"! There is no more grievous sin than harsh preaching and the drubbing of the faithful in the pretext that the preacher is the only one with access to spiritual vision. As John Donne reminded us long ago, "No man is an island . . . each man's death diminishes me."[6] Paul wrote, "If one part suffers, every part suffers with it" (1 Cor. 12:26). Thomas Merton wrote, "Christian personalism is then the sacramental sharing of personality in the mystery of life. This sharing demands full respect for the mystery of the person, whether it be our own person, or the person of our neighbor, or the infinite secret of God."[7] His life, fully born in us, will leave us with total respect for all persons.

Second, the painful conclusion of this truth is that not all will receive our sermons as we would like. The subject of our proclamation may find itself the focus of gossip. Neither Christ (under the attack of the Pharisees) nor Paul (under the slur of the Corinthians) failed to respect the personhood of his defamers. Without a profound respect for persons, the ministry of the pastor degenerates into a tyranny of some sort.

The preacher must allow the God of his devotional life the freedom to be unpredictable. Perhaps the reason that the Holy Spirit does not "land" more regularly in our churches is that the runways are stacked with ecclesiastical agenda. Many preachers are zealous to grant God this freedom, but their zeal is tamed just by administering the program of the church. The notion that God might change time-honored forms or denominational structures is unsettling. My suspicion is that the only sure evidence that God is really present in a sermon is whether or not the sermon strokes the status quo (as someone once pointed out, status quo is Latin for "the mess we're in") or challenges it. "Thus-saith-the-Lord" preaching orders the church to do the work of God by putting spiritual force into ecclesiology. Restructuring the church to make room for the Spirit is an evidence that God may be truly involved in what we are doing.

As I said in the introduction, renovation is always painful. My first pastorate was a challenge. I had begun the church, and after some years of hard work, we built a building. I considered the building part of my life project. I felt, though never said, that the building would be there long after I was gone, indicating that God had once been at work in my life. Now, of course, they have a new pastor, and he is leading the church to sell the building I struggled so hard to build. My inwardness was bruised. I had gotten possessive with the mere physical evidences of my ministry.

Feelings of possessiveness about our calling cause us to forget that we are not on our own to measure life and its accomplishments in terms of ourselves. Furthermore, possessiveness squelches our desire to let the Spirit have free rein in the church. Most churches sing, "Holy Spirit, breathe on me," but in fact do not want him breathing down their necks. So in reality, they sing, "Come, Holy Spirit—but leave the machinery intact!" Such grasping ecclesiology puts ourselves in the control tower and God in a holding pattern. It does not clear the congestion from our runways so that the Spirit can touch down. Furthermore, these feelings of possessiveness frustrate the preacher (sometimes all through life) because he is never able to synchronize what he wants for his church and the personal courage it takes to make that happen.

The preacher who lives in touch with God cannot help but be labeled a nonconformist. He doesn't mean to be, but at the center of his life stands a nonconformist God behaving in his customary manner. Naturally the preacher gets the blame for all the innovation inspired by God. The result is sometimes congregational upheaval, a landslide of criticism. This upheaval often increases the mystery, and the Sunday crowds grow (while some leave). The sensitive preacher will always feel some agony because of the Spirit's disturbing presence (it is never easy to lose people), but the issue is not how well the preacher holds it all together but rather how the church is subject unto Christ.

The key is that the genuine man or woman of God never enjoys hurting others, nor making people angry. Hostility is often the grievous by-product of the preacher's necessary pleasure (the kingdom of God), but it is never the goal. The kingdom of God has never been equated with personal comfort or business as usual in any institution. The result of the reign of Christ is always glory, but those who desire the reign (not the glory) will see the church born in power. The resulting intrigue will be continual renewal. The preacher cannot achieve this, but he will be at the center of the intrigue, reminding communicants of the source.

The Silent Center

It is never the preacher's excessive speaking that is the key to this intrigue. In our naiveté, we who preach may have been first drawn to our career for egoistic reasons. The attraction may have been an elitist desire that tempted our personal weakness toward authority. We may have envisioned how it would be to hold an audience in sway by being clever or authoritative or emotive. We may even have felt it would be wonderful having others celebrate us. These illusions quickly evaporated after a board meeting or two in our first church.

The oral side of our career is most visible, but it is never the source of spiritual power. In fact, our devotional life (of which we have already spoken) is the secret of real clout. A friend of mine long ago reminded me that I could not *help* people if I was always *with* people. It was a wise insight hidden from me then. Now I understand. When Harold Fickett Jr. says, "A preacher is the epic poet of his people,"[8] we must admit that the epic gains its form from silence.

People listen to, react to, criticize, or compliment the oral side of our lives, however. The sermon is, therefore, the most important of all speeches to be heard in any community. Still, when it comes from the silent center of our lives, we will likely not be so complimented. David Mains conjectures that probably no one went up to Jesus after the Sermon on the Mount and said, "Liked your talk a lot, Jesus! . . . It was a blessing!"[9] From the silence of our devotional life comes such strong words that the best comment by the congregation is inner wrangling and sorting and furious alignment or dissension. Sermons that change lives rarely receive compliments. Their work of dialogue is still going on as the believer leaves church.

Sermon compliments are often ego fodder, and preaching for compliments is the smallest of pursuits. Preaching from the silent center is the evidence that we who preach on trust are also living it. Preaching, in one sense, merely discharges the firearm that God has loaded in the silent place. The successful volley does not mean that we have passed homiletics but rather that we have been with God.

A biographer of Archbishop François de Fénelon observed: "Simple and orderly living was the secret of his power and efficiency, for his austerity was in reality a purposeful and rational expenditure rather than a self-conscious mortification. It represented the beauty of an orderly and clean mind that naturally turned away from gaudy gewgaws and the disorder of the unnecessary."[10]

T. S. Eliot may have been writing in another context, but all that he insinuated is true: "Against the Word the unstilled world still whirled / About the centre of the silent Word."[11] It is this silent Word that makes the sermon word effective, and the depth our sermons achieve reflects this silent Word.

In the proverbial hurricane of church life, the quietest place in our lives remains the eye of the storm, the silent center. In this place of self-imposed solitude, no communication is possible except that with God. The sermonic ideal is to talk from the silent center of the preacher to the silent center of those who attend the sermon. Such communication is strenuous and exhausting. Still, we cannot look into the faces of communicants and tell whether their silent centers are really all that silent. The average pew-sitter is filled with turmoil. Some statistics suggest that more than half of those who enter the congregation are experiencing some kind of inner storm. They are hurricanes without eyes, walking storms with no silence at the center of their troubled lives.

The sermon's longing is not just to speak to the quiet heart but to quiet the noise in the busy heart. In such lives, noise is so dominant that the verbiage of the sermon may only add to the noise and confusion of inner voices. The sermon needs to counsel all to be quiet, to know that God is (Ps. 46:10).

One of the most refreshing movements of our day is the growing resurgence of interest in the inner life among Protestants. Christ-formation is now a concern in most seminary curricula. May the movement pave the way to the future, with the people of God made serious by a listening spirit. In such a new day, the sermon may at last know the glory of moving from silent center to silent center, and the kingdom of God may be once again "at hand" (Matt. 3:2 KJV).

The Compulsion of Mystery

If mystery's soul is silence, then compulsion is its life. Mystery dogs our restless hearts, compelling investigation. Things do not "go bump in the night" for long without being explored. Sermons in touch with the Spirit will not long remain unexamined in the pulpit. They draw the mind like an unopened package begging to be explored.

For 185 hours at Asbury College in 1970, a church service refused to end, and the intrigue of a nation turned toward a small Kentucky town. An observer wrote, "There is no human vocabulary that can capture the full dimension of one divine movement. . . . Those of us who were there can never look upon the things of the world quite the same."[12] The revivals of Goforth in China or the Canadian revival at Saskatchewan (Saskatoon) are examples of the same kind of compelling mystery that draws our attention. Even Jonathan Edwards wrote of the 1735 revival in Northampton, Massachusetts, "The town seemed to be full of the presence of God. It never was so full of love, nor so full of joy, and yet so full of distress, as it was then."[13]

The mysterious moving of God might be best described as a kind of divine takeover that leaves us in wonder rather than in charge. I am also a novelist. In my acquaintance with other novelists, I have found a consensus of opinion that suggests that the novel has a life of its own. There is a moment in the writing of novels when the story takes charge and we who write are nearly as dumbfounded by our newfound observer status as those who buy our novels.

In a sense, the Spirit of God knows those special moments of freedom when he is unleashed (always by willing men and women) to move as he might. At such moments, the church and its programs are all servant to the movement. Not only do the program and people yield up direction, but the sermon itself becomes a servant. The sermon bows its homiletical head; it is no longer the show-off centerpiece, but a quiet beholder. It remains there, but only as the tool of other forces from other worlds.

The Spirit never comes as the result of sermon preparation, he comes as a result of the soul's desire. No area of church life is left untouched by this desire. God must be free, and only as he is set free to move in every direction of human improvement does he come at all.

I started this book convinced that a section on the Spirit was important because we evangelicals do not want to preach any sermon (we say) without the Spirit's direct involvement. I think, in the writing of this book, I have come to see why: Few books on preaching give much space to the Spirit. It is altogether difficult to talk about the *sermon qua sermon* and, at the same time, to talk about abandoning the sermon's almighty importance to allow the renovating, uncontrollable Spirit freedom from the structuring of preparation. Still, there can be no denying that when the preacher understands not just the place of the sermon in worship but also the place for the Spirit in the renovating work on the human condition, the church is ready for its best transforming work. This transformation comes not from desiring to preach well (which is a good desire), but from making the sermon an instrument rather than a showpiece.

Heavy structuring is no more a threat to the coming of the Spirit than sloppy, undisciplined sermon preparation. Consider this warning, all you tempted to let sermon preparation diminish in the interest of being unstructured: God's work in the sermon does not diminish ours. Instead, our work will grow into ever more difficult areas. For besides the exegesis, outlining, and developing of the sermon, we must add the harder work of waiting, seeking, and agonizing. We must prepare as though there were no Holy Spirit and then preach as though everything utterly depended on him. To be used of the Spirit, our preparation should be done with his ends in mind. Then our delivery will not be like drying clay—too hard, at last, for his fingers to fashion.

How can we get a handle on this, the more numinous side of sermon preparation? Spiritual discipline is ever important to the coming of the Spirit, but there is the inevitable, uncontrollable issue of his coming. "Surprise" is his word! Charles Finney describes his conversion thus: "All my feelings seemed to rise and flow out and the utterance of my heart was: 'I want to pour out my soul to God.'" He rushed into a back room of the office to pray, and then it happened:

> There was no fire, no light in the room; nevertheless it appeared to me as if it were perfectly light. As I went in and shut the door after me, it seemed as if I met the Lord Jesus Christ face to face. It did not occur to me then, nor did it for some time afterward, that it was a wholly mental state. On the contrary, it seemed to me that I saw Him as I would see any other man. He said nothing, but looked at me in such a manner as to break me down right at His feet . . . it seemed to me a reality that He stood before me and I fell down at His feet and poured out my soul to Him. I wept aloud like a child, and made such confessions as I could with a choked utterance. It seemed to me that I bathed His feet with tears, and yet I had no distinct impression that I touched Him.[14]

Two things must be pointed out from Finney's conversion that are typical of the Spirit, namely, the elements of surprise encounter and utter emotion. Preaching and the act of worship are often set up to miss the Spirit's coming. In the first place, many evangelical churches are afraid of emotion. Could this fear be behind some of our severe liturgy? Is it a kind of "beating on the pans" to drive away the wolves of Pentecostalism? Would we rather leave worship starched of heart than risk our reputation to emotional wildfire?

The element of surprise is equally fearsome. We don't want any surprises in worship. Spontaneity is a frightening idea. Surprise unnerves us and wilts our best-outlined manuscripts, which we carefully prepared to unfold the genius of our study. Jesus said that the elusive Spirit is like the wind: "You cannot tell where it comes from or where it is going. So it is with everyone born of the Spirit" (John 3:8). It is precisely this uncontrollable aspect of the new birth that we may have attempted to control.

As a metaphor of salvation, new birth implies that life is about to issue from some spiritual womb. Birth, although it announces its coming months before it arrives, knows no predictable moment. The entire medical realm is forced continually to deal with the possibility of surprise. In our congregation through the years, babies have been born suddenly, without warning—at home, in squad cars, or in ambulances. Unborn babies seem to have a life-moment of their own. "So it is," said Christ, "with everyone born of the Spirit."

May preaching learn to be wise. It was never meant to learn an exactness which demanded that its delivery be the same on all occasions—emotionless, sterile, and under a human thumb. The unconventional worship forms of the new neo-Pentecostals may have much to teach the rest of us. Some might object here and say, "Please, please! What about our dignity, our tradition, the liturgies of our founders?" Even so, one can, in Pentecostal churches, see two issues clearly: First, God is welcome when and however he comes; and second, emotion is the footprint of the Savior's passing.

Conclusion

However we worship, if there is no compulsion beyond our planning and sermon writing, we will not only miss the coming of the Spirit, we will not communicate the reality of Jesus very well. For Jesus and the Spirit are both of the godhead, and to exclude one from our preachment and our worship is to exclude the other. In the heart of the pastor who is sensitive to the calling of Christ, nothing matters but Christ's pleasure, and that pleasure is a haunting compulsion. A student once remarked, "I can't get Jesus Christ out of my mind. If I dismiss him as an idea, he haunts me as a person. If I dismiss him as a person, he haunts me as an idea."[15] May such a spirit haunt our worship and our preaching. Should this spirit come to us, may preachers not cling to the science of homiletics and miss the coming of him who created sermons in the first place. Always as he comes, we will marry strong study and preparation to the freedom of God.

In this chapter, I am trying to open preaching to its fullest destiny, a double freedom. Study and preparation will set us free to teach with content and power, but a strong devotional life will enable us to understand that the longing of God is the reclamation of the human race. Homiletics, at its heart, is a casual word meaning "chat." In point of fact, for some it has come to mean "inviolable lecture." I wanted to begin this book with a plea for God to be as welcome in our services as our sermons. If, at the outset, we seek a marriage of spirit and mind, of study and inwardness, of discipline and spontaneity, of professionalism and sensitivity, of holding in and letting go, then our sermons will be more than sermons. They will become the beckoning finger of God in the lives of people. This is the fullest possibility of preaching. We should settle for no other.

2

The Spirit as Teacher

An eloquent man must speak so as to teach, to delight, and to persuade. To teach is a necessity, to delight is a beauty, to persuade is a triumph.

Cicero

After the speaker had droned on for some forty minutes, [a man] met a friend coming in. The man asked, "Am I very late, Zeke? What's he talking about?"
"Don't know. He ain't said yet!"

Tim Timmons

If a man should claim to have had a vision of God which did not bring him to penitence, I should feel very sure that he had had no real vision, or that it was not a vision of the real God.

William Temple

From the time the umbilical cord is severed, learning begins; to be alive is to learn. Yet I have often had the vague impression that learning ceases when the sermon begins. Christian conversion welcomes the Holy Spirit as teacher. In the Spirit's presence, God enters into league with our learning nature. Jesus taught that the Holy Spirit

41

would be our teacher to guide us into all truth (John 16:13), and that instruction of the Spirit comes from within.

Herein is a great paradox of life in the Spirit. The indwelling teacher waits for the word of the sermon. It is as though the coming of outer sermonic truth and the inner Spirit of truth both bear witness that we are the children of God (Rom. 8:16). When we pick up the Bible and let its print encounter our retinas, the words travel "optic-nerve-wise" to the wondrous storage and retrieval system of our minds. The same thing happens when we pick up a chemistry book. The difference is that chemistry knows no inner instructor.

The preacher is a kind of golden link between his own inner teacher and the inner teacher of each of his communicants. The sermon, then, becomes the word that passes from mind to mind and from spirit to spirit. In this sense, the sermon, from first to last, is not a speech. Speeches cannot enter the realm of great mystery that is preaching.

The great teachings of the Spirit of God address these five ideas—mystery, true reality, God's demands, ultimate reckoning, and God's self-disclosure. It is this last idea, the idea of God's self-disclosure, that makes the sermon the special document of each member of the congregation.

Teaching the Unteachable

Since we have already dealt with the intrigue of this mystery of preaching, let me remind every preacher of the sermon's obligation to be centered in the glory of the inscrutable God. Yet how can we teach what is so mentally elusive as the mystery of God? We dare not teach in a matter-of-fact, earthbound mode, for the sermon must portray to all who hear it that we have broken the shackles of ordinary earthly logic and academic systems. The sermon must admit that we are teaching things that must always remain partly hidden. If we fail to communicate this, we are not his people imbued with that otherworldliness which we discussed in chapter 1. If our teaching is shackled by logic, we will leave the sermon too earthbound to help the earth. The sermon must be the gatekeeper, refusing to admit the hucksters of secularism into the ideal values of the church.

How do we wed the Holy Spirit to catechism? We cannot be a people of the Spirit without containing the Spirit. It seems foolish to suggest that man, the secularist—having already walked on the moon, eliminated smallpox, and engineered incredible accomplishments—could be filled with the extraterrestrial Spirit of God.

Within the given parameters of mystery, the sermon must teach; it must catechize, present lessons, argue for doctrinal purity, and quicken the mind with enlightenment. Without this teaching, both mystery and uniqueness are absent from the faith. Also gone is the invitation to believe the unbelievable. Faith can only live as long as it remains unexplainable.

Few sermons will dwell on the mystery of the Spirit, but that mystery is ever the underlying presupposition. It is like a man submitting himself to a heart surgeon. He neither expects nor wants the surgeon to state his credentials, but underlying the grave business of surgery, he knows that the surgeon is more than meets an unstudied eye. The surgeon contains within himself a complexity that remains untried by the trusting patient.

The teaching of the sermon must mix the most saving, redeeming values into such bulky paradoxes as atonement or election and free will. The teaching will seem too mystical to matter in the hard-core world of executive finance, for instance. The Trinity defies all rationality. As teaching unfolds in mystery, the teacher will see it in the rapt faces of the students. The energy of holy communication will charge the atmosphere! The sermon is activated by ions of the inscrutable that bind us in the thrall of captive irrationality.

Preparing: Our Work and His Work

Consider the mandate we have just examined: Solid instruction and the preacher's devotional life are not in contradiction. Living with both God and our people is our double obligation. Life on these two levels will guide us into knowing what the sermon should teach.

As we live in two modes, we must see in two. We must behold the Spirit as unknowable mystery and as great pragmatist. This means he will speak on topics that are beneficial to those who attend. The seminarian who stands up to address his sleepy congregation on the implications of supralapsarianism in the work-a-day world obviously is not prepared to teach with relevance or authority. Such sermons are preached by those who have let the world of ideas close them off from the world of people and from the agenda of God in the world at hand. The teaching sermon begins in the heart of the pastor whose touch with God spawns usable truth.

In the formative moments of a sermon, preachers should ask these questions:

What is the need of the congregation?

What does the Bible have to say about this need?

What life experiences have I had and what literary insights can I glean from books that might help illuminate the scriptural help I can offer?

How can I break the subject down into understandable units that the congregation can most easily grasp?

These questions are the best, most powerful part of our preaching. Without asking them, the sermon is dead before it ever begins to live. These four items should be pre-preparation! That is, these insights come first in the process of preparation. They are so basic that they cannot even be called study.

These questions, like Kipling's six honest serving men (what, why, when, how, where, who)[1] can be our guides. They are simple interrogatives that fix understanding into sermon preparation. Cicero long ago marked the path of clarity in all public speaking:

Determine exactly what you should say.

Arrange the material in proper order.

Clothe the speech with well-crafted words and incisive sentences.

Fix the speech in your mind.

Deliver the speech with dignity and grace.[2]

Let us not blame the Holy Spirit for poor preaching when we are slipshod in our preparation. Having known preachers who sat down on Saturday night after their favorite television program and hastily prepared for Sunday, I have wondered that the Holy Spirit does not abandon the church altogether. Often these very types adamantly insist on not quenching the Spirit with overpreparation. Their lives are the mockery of their doctrine. Some, in arguing with formally studied sermons, say, "The early church fathers depended solely upon the Spirit for their sermons," as though this is an argument for abandoning preparation altogether. It is true that in many evangelistic churches the results of the uninformed, spontaneous sermon are dramatic, but those who flatter themselves that laziness is the confirmation of God's presence in the sermon are dangerously naive.

Robert Louis Stevenson is reported to have said, "I . . . sit a long while silent on my eggs."[3] Brooding over thought and study consistently hatches better sermons, but, as in the hatchery, brooding over infertile thinking or slovenly study produces nothing. Incubating the sermon encompasses both formal and informal brooding. The informal brooding comes largely before any specific thoughts are set on paper, but formal brooding is the fertile kind. Formal brooding is the process of carrying the sermon in mind for several days or (in the case of special occasion sermons) for several weeks between the time it is outlined and the time it is delivered. The sermon that is early given this primordial thought shape will grow in fullness by simply being carried around in the mind while it grows in power and substance.

If the teaching Spirit is to create lessons of power from the sermon, simplicity must rule. The sermon must never try to teach too much. One evidence that the Holy Spirit is involved in the process of the teaching will depend upon how simple the sermon remains in its concepts. Surely the Spirit, who inspired Paul to write, "Let all things be done decently and in order" (1 Cor. 14:40 KJV), would not champion a sermon whose diversity prevents focus.

Helmut Thielicke warns that those who try to set forth too many diverse truths within the same sermon are often guilty of blinding with light: "We are the moles who have just crawled out of the ground and we can stand the light of only a small candle. . . . But you descend upon us with the floodlight of all the truths of the centuries. . . . Please, just one candle, one single candle!"[4] Luther also chides those who clutter simple truth with meandering trivia: "[Theirs is] the art in which nobody sticks to the text. . . . [Unless] the Spirit himself speaks through the preachers . . . we shall again have sermons on [trivial subjects]."[5]

Further, we complicate the Spirit's teaching when our illustrations glob together without strong separating precepts. Illustrations must never fly at such a pace that the focus is obscured. Focus is also lost in long quotations. There is always danger that the words of others brought to our sermon will stifle logic by their sheer numbers.

Preaching True Reality

True reality is spiritual reality, eternal and unchanging. The teaching Spirit is the only access to this heightened reality. It is interesting to note that Jesus' Sermon on the Mount, along with the sermons of Peter and Stephen, are more than sermons. They are, in a sense, theological apologetics set out to explain unexplainable things. Jesus, for instance, makes clear in the Sermon on the Mount the true realities of heaven and hell. We cannot live in the material world making moral and temporal decisions until we have faced the final (and real) end of all our choices. The things Jesus states in his sermon are the furthest extensions of true reality. Elusive as this reality is, it is the preface to understanding our immediate existence.

Peter, on the day of Pentecost, saw the nature of this reality. True reality meant that Christ, who was the Lord of Glory, had been crucified (Acts 2:36). Peter made it clear that all must repent and be baptized (Acts 2:38), for having come to an understanding of true reality, they were under obligation to act. Stephen's sermon, like

Peter's, told the real truth that Jesus was the Messiah (Acts 7:52) and demanded repentance at the center of institutional Judaism.

In the case of all three of these sermons, none of the listeners were allowed to hold to their supposed view of things in the face of true reality. This is the sermon's onus, its inescapable burden, to challenge secondary reality. In the very act of standing to preach, every preacher is an apologist, championing reality in its purest form. Confronting popular views of material reality, the preacher will often translate as devoted but naive. So the calling of the pastor is to live with the obligation of his calling, whatever his reputation.

Addressing true reality calls for tough rhetoric. The Spirit will provide the energy for our apologetic and so make strong the teaching of the sermon. Our calling is to defend the gospel as we confront our culture. Our sermons, therefore, must call the secularly entrenched world to break its tether with killing rationality. One has only to examine the sermons of John the Baptist or Chrysostom or John Calvin to see that the sternest use of sermonic image calls to those ensnared by logic, "Hear these important words . . . they are life!"

John Calvin spoke in an almost abusive manner and "called opponents 'asses, pigs, riffraff, dogs, idiots, [and] stinking beasts.'" Likewise, Reformation preachers of his ilk found themselves humiliated, exiled, and sometimes burned at the stake. Still, they used caustic language to demand attention. One Reformation scholar writes of Calvin: "Instead of saying, 'I blame,' he said, 'I spit in his face.' Instead of, 'I am wrong,' 'I deserve to have my face spit upon.' Instead of saying, 'The Lord spurns those ceremonies,' 'It is as though He spat upon all those services.' Instead of saying, 'Perverse human nature,' 'Each one would scratch out his neighbor's eyes.'"[6] Jonathan Edwards also ignored the God of butterflies in favor of the God "who held sinners over hell as one might hold a spider over the fire."[7]

There are two dangers of using such forceful language in the contemporary sermon. Such language puts listeners into a bristling, defensive posture which impedes their ability to receive. Such scalding terminology may cause unbelievers to feel that they have been ambushed.

A second danger, however, may be even greater. The preacher cannot maintain an angry profile of continual confrontation and expect to relate to those who live in the world at hand. The preacher who translates as being altogether otherworldly will be isolated from those who still think that even if the world does end in flame, it's okay to go bowling on Friday nights.

I would like to be able to say that the preacher who is castigated for being heavenly minded is enduring a noble form of martyrdom. Not so! The pastor who hides behind a wall of stern reprisals and derogating "heaven-itis" will be miserable, and his attendance will be sparse. Our otherworldliness must be kept in balance with our desire for popcorn. Smile during the sermon. It will ward off the demons of hyperseriousness.

The teaching Spirit seems never to be mentioned in Scripture without an emphasis on joy. Indeed, Whitsunday dawns with such spiritual joy that the local townspeople believe the witnesses to be full of wine and good times (Acts 2:13). Paul contends that sermonizers should be inebriates of joy (Eph. 5:18–19). A sermon entirely void of joy is probably not Spirit driven; God does not make gray his coming. Indeed, the martyr who said, "Joy is the most infallible proof of the presence of God," spoke the truth. Laughter is the generous footprint of joy in sermons made bold by the Spirit of life.

When I find myself becoming gray with the Holy Spirit, I intentionally break the cathexis I feel with the world of the Spirit. Cathexis is, of course, the label that psychologists give to emotional attachment. If I am locked into condemnation and harsh preaching, it is time for me to paint a picture or read a book (on anything but Calvinism, at such a moment). I break with intensity so I can preach without excessive condemnation.

Charles Finney once reminded all Christians of this great truth: "A *censorious spirit* is conclusive evidence of a backslidden heart. . . . It is a state of mind that reveals itself in harsh judgments, harsh sayings, and the manifestation of uncomfortable feelings toward individuals. This state of mind is entirely incompatible with a loving heart."[8] This must certainly be true of the pastor. The loving heart may know seasons of rebuke, but, overall, preachers (and especially pastors) must live and preach in relationship.

We must not forget the heavy truth that Christians who preach peace with too much emphasis on otherworldliness betray themselves. So often at the heart of harsh precept preaching stands a peaceless preacher and church. Hazel Motes, Flannery O'Connor's street preacher, has our number as he shouts, "There's no peace for the redeemed . . . and I preach peace, . . . the Church Without Christ, the church peaceful and satisfied!"[9] Everything is a matter of balance; the cathexis of the preacher locked up in this world is as unforgivable as that of the preacher so divorced from humanity that *his* humanity is in question.

Rhetoric alone will not convince our listeners that the spiritual world is the enduring one. Mystery is not an oral argument; mystery is an aura. It is sermonic light, seen, not heard, so that those who attend the sermon know that there is more to the indwelling Spirit than the senses can measure.

The Demand of God

Two of the main sources for this authority are the Bible and the indwelling Spirit. Strong pulpit authority is up for grabs today. There seems among some to be a question as to whether or not the pulpit is the place for authority. Preaching in the "indicative" is often favored over preaching in the "imperative," but the Spirit and the Word always couple to produce unquestionable authority. If it was a compliment to Jesus when the people said, "He taught . . . as one having authority, and not as the scribes" (Matt. 7:29 KJV), we can assume that authority is a quality of preaching that the sermon dare not abandon.

Authority is a sign of the Spirit's presence in the sermon, but remember, no preacher should translate as heavy-handed. Rather, let the Spirit bear both the word and the authority. Let preachers be responsible for according dignity to all men and women while the Spirit remains in charge of authority. Then the sermon's authority will emanate from something other than our own ego needs or opinions.

The idea of the demand of God is fundamental to the entire Hebrew-Christian tradition. God's demand is the subject of the Holy

Spirit and the sermon. The preacher's job is not only to state that demand, but also to use the best technique of sermon preparation to illuminate it and make it clear.

Beware this double pitfall: First, the demand of God must never translate as the demand of the preacher. Second, the demand of God in a relational day and age does not need to be soft-pedaled to be effective; it should, however, be presented in relational terms. God is not such an important concept to modern listeners that his demands will be instantly welcome. Any spiritual demand in our relational age is likely to meet with resistance. This is true whether the listener sees it as coming from God or not. Our day has become so relational that all forms of authority are seen as arbitrary.

The demand of God is key, but it must be heralded within the framework of sound reason. Isaiah wrote, "Come now, let us reason together" (Isa. 1:18). The Scriptures say that Paul reasoned with the Thessalonian Jews out of the Scriptures (Acts 17:2). Is reasoning soft-pedaling the demand of God? No. Compromise is out of the question. The glory of the sermon and the preacher is the dialogue that makes the mandate both heard and effective.

God and Ultimate Reckoning

Biblical preaching is always set within an apocalyptic framework. Heaven and hell are constant themes in Scripture. Almost no book of the New Testament ignores the ultimate reckoning of the second coming. Most of the time, the second coming is presented as sudden and secret, thief-like! From one generation to the next, the church has survived with this immediacy still intact.

Conclusion

Early Christians were filled with the Holy Spirit (Acts 2:4; 4:31), and every Christian is commanded to be filled with the Spirit (Eph. 5:18), to walk in the Spirit (Gal. 5:16 KJV), to mortify the deeds of the body through the Spirit (Rom. 8:13 KJV), and never to grieve (Eph. 4:30) or quench the Spirit (1 Thess. 5:19 KJV). Above all, we are to be led by the Spirit (Rom. 8:14).

The Spirit is the evidence of God's presence in both the preacher and the congregation. There is no church without him. David Brainerd was said by those who knew him to pray for the coming of the Spirit upon his work. Battling tuberculosis, he prayed through the harsh New England winters that God would indeed send revival. It happened suddenly in 1745: "The power of God seemed to descend on the assembly 'like a rushing mighty wind' and with an astonishing energy bore all down before it. I stood amazed at the influence that seized the audience . . . the irresistible force of a mighty torrent."[10]

Brainerd's example makes it clear that the preacher should always seek the Spirit's leadership. With his leadership, both the authority and the content of the sermon can focus on Christ. This not only honors the Spirit, but ensures that both our apologetic and exhortation will be fruitful. Focused on Christ, the listener will see the panorama of the well-organized sermon. Christ himself will provide the light that illuminates both the instruction and the authority. In that generous illumination, the unseen things of God are made visible and usable. The preacher who clearly sees Christ will be able to project him on the screen of other searching lives.

3

The Spirit as Counselor

Preach to the suffering, and you will never lack a congregation.

Joseph Parker

This means *thinking with them*. . . . Another helpful activity is to *speak frequently in secular situations*. . . . I must also *play with them*. . . . Fourth, I must *counsel with them*.

Tim Timmons

From the Cathedral of the Perpetual Smile to First Happy Baptist, there are plenty of people who would mistakenly have us believe that the life of faith is basically one long joyride. To sustain this illusion and the quest for the Holy Grin, they transform the church program into a religious amusement park hawking a thrill-a-minute, fun-filled experience, complete with emotional roller coasters, religious variety shows, verbal trick mirrors, and more. Such teaching is a half-truth at best, a shoddy imitation of authentic joy in faith.

Howard R. Macy

The sermon has sometimes been described as personal counseling on a group basis. Counselors are the ministers of disentanglement—facilitators, therefore, of self-discovery. They tackle the hard questions and so unlock our souls. The sermon is counsel. Christ said that the Holy Spirit would come as a counselor (John 16:5–7). The Christ who left his disciples on the Mount of Olives at the ascension left his newly created church somewhat in doubt, loneliness, and bereavement. His Holy Spirit was to comfort the church in the physical absence of her Lord, as a hand on the shoulder of the grieving church.

Christ was not dead, but his absence was debilitating. The Holy Spirit came like the Quaker who offered his presence to a bereaved friend, saying, "I know no words to speak to thee, but I am with thee in the grieving silence." The sermon should grapple with what C. S. Lewis called "the problem of pain": If God is good, he should want us to be happy. If he is God, he has the power to make us happy. Since we are broken with the agony of life, God must either be powerless or not good.[1]

The grappling sermon may sound more muddled than we would like, but its willingness to struggle says that the Spirit and the sermon are joined in a counseling ministry. As we observed earlier, many of those who enter our churches from week to week are broken in spirit. They have either had or soon will have a wrangling affair with doubt. From time to time they cannot find God. If they do find him, they cannot tell if he is good or weak. They sit down in the pew, wrangling over the ultimate meaning of life while the sermon flies about them, and their doubt holds counsel with hope. They sit and beg for any line upon which to hang meaning in the heaviness of their turmoil. In the shredding of their being, there is a kind of double hope, the sermon and the Spirit.

The sermon we have identified in another place as the speech (*sermo, sermonis*), and the Spirit we now identify as counselor, *parakletos* in Greek. The counselor, *parakletos,* is a compound word in Greek. It means, "one called alongside," or "to be in the company of." The entire ministry of the Holy Spirit is that of one called alongside in the absence of another. This powerful Greek idea lies beneath the glorious ministry of the Spirit.

Now let us ask ourselves here at the outset, "Why do people come to church?" I wish my people came to glean the scholarship of my seminary years, but, honestly, I believe they come for sociological reasons. They are hungry to meet and to know. "All meeting," as Martin Buber reminds us, "is living." To be in a community is to know life, says M. Scott Peck in *A Different Drum*. "When I am with a group of human beings . . . through both the agony and the joy of community, I have a dim sense that I am participating in a phenomenon for which there is only one word . . . 'glory.'"[2] If, indeed, people are enduring sermons to get at community, perhaps unwittingly we have discovered the marvelous correlation of the Spirit and the sermon. The Spirit is company—yes, even constant, indwelling company—and therefore in community with God. The sermon is the focal part of our common celebration, the center of our community as the body of Christ (1 Cor. 12:27).

The Spirit and the sermon join forces as an answer to the problem of pain. Both A. P. Gibbs and Fred Craddock have illustrated the meaning of worship with similar parables. Both tell stories of a pet, abused, mistreated, forsaken, cold, and alone. The pet is taken home by a loving family and kept overnight, then, through compassion, kept forever. In the keeping of the pet, it grows in health, weight, and, of course, love. In the Gibbs illustration, the animal is a dog, who, after being restored to health by a loving master, walks to his master's chair one night. The master is aware of a gentle lick on his hand. He looks down and sees the one-time mongrel, looking up with gratitude. What the restored and loved dog is feeling, says Gibbs, is worship.[3] The Spirit and the sermon produce worship, a chance for the lonely to be the restored and the dispossessed to be overwhelmed with gratitude.

Sermonizing Counsel

There is no such thing as remote comfort. All true comfort is near, and generally near enough to touch. In *The Table of Inwardness*, I spend a great deal of time trying to establish a case for spiritual intimacy. We must be touched by God. All great revivals from Reformation times to the present have been characterized by fearless sermons, quickened by the intimate touch of the Spirit.

The emotion that we discussed in chapter 2 comes back into play at this point. When the counsel of the Spirit finds voice in the sermon, people will be affected emotionally. I twice have preached on human sexuality and the expectation of God. I did not attempt to get people to weep. I attempted to tell the truth about the sexual ghosts that often haunt multiple marriages and the deep human longing to be forgiven in life. At the conclusion of both sermons, many were so broken in spirit, they wept their way to the altar, seeking the counsel of God.

There is ever a temptation here toward emotional neurosis. Emotion may breed emotion. I certainly am not advocating the entreating of feeling as an indication that we are serious with God. We must decide that adoration, not feeling, is the goal of worship. To drive directly for emotional togetherness breeds the temptation to fake it. If we are not careful, we will at last trump up what we originally set out to achieve as the by-product of honest dialogical preaching. Emotion alone is a cheap substitute for adoration.

Remember this: dialogue is the language of two. If the sermon is the voice of dialogue, it is only one half of the conversation. The congregation supplies the other half. Their half is not oral, but if it is not real, there is no meeting of the minds, no involvement of the Spirit!

Often the sermon is unheard in times of either great turmoil or ease. Someone asked J. C. Penney what were the two greatest motivators in his life; he answered in four words, "Jesus Christ and adversity."[4] It is often our need for the former and our desire to be free of the latter that brings us to church. The sermon devoid of the Spirit quickly grows captive to fixed styles set within the framework of rigid worship. Such preaching may contain only ponderous, predictable truths heard as nonconfrontational droning. By contrast, the sermon that is free and enlivened by the Spirit is incisive, cutting through predictability to sustain the needy with true spiritual security.

The sermon and the Spirit always work in combination to pronounce liberation. Sometimes the Spirit and sermon do supply direct answers to human need, but most often they answer indirectly. Most problems are not solved by listening to sermons. The sermon, no matter how sincere, cannot solve these unsolvable problems. So if the sermon is not a problem solver, where shall we go for solutions? Together with the Spirit, the sermon exists to point out that having answers is not essential to living. What is essential is the sense of God's presence during dark seasons of questioning. The Spirit is the best illuminator of one truth: There may be more important issues than those immediate problems that brought us to church in the first place. Our need for specific answers is dissolved in the greater issue of the lordship of Christ over all questions—those that have answers and those that don't.

If most people who come into church with heavy needs leave carrying the same burdens, what then is the value of the church? The church cannot eliminate the heaviness of life, but God strengthens backs when he does not lighten loads. Like Paul, the burdened listeners can then say, "While I still have my problems, I now 'reckon that the sufferings of this present time are not worthy to be compared with the glory which shall be'" (Rom. 8:18 KJV).

This enlightening work of the Spirit takes the load off! Charles Finney said that the sermon "breaks the power of the world and of sin."[5] This may seem an oversimplification, but intimacy grows between those who have seen the proper relationship between the size of God and the not-so-overwhelming size of their own problems.

The preacher must ever be willing to give the Holy Spirit credit for all sermonic success. For some sermons may appear to succeed when the Holy Spirit has not come near them; others may appear to fail when they are replete with his presence. It is a mistake to read our moods as the sole indicators of the Spirit's presence in our words. "When preachers have flat Sundays, as every preacher does, and begin boring themselves with their own sermons, it is not a sign of the Spirit's absence; . . . Likewise, when words seem to tumble from our lips, spinning in wild flights of poetic wonder, it is not a sign of the Spirit's presence; . . . The Spirit labors as much in our struggles as in our spontaneities."[6] How wise is David Buttrick's assessment. Sheep

57

and shepherd comprise the community, and as the community is both vulnerable and disciplined, the Spirit comes.

Every shepherd is also a sheep! Since shepherding is our calling, we must speak to the sheep, but first, last, and always, we are one with them. The Spirit will not attend arrogant papalism in the pulpit. To play the all-sufficient counselor is to act alone in the sermon. The preacher is but one sinner telling another where to get forgiveness, one beggar telling another where to get bread, one leper waiting with others for the touch of the Great Physician. Accepting our calling as divine without selling ourselves that way prepares the way of the Lord.

The vulnerable shepherd preaching to the wounded sheep is the goal of the counselor Spirit. I remember one Sunday, in relating my joy at someone's conversion, I broke into tears. I felt embarrassed, for I have said so often, "A great preacher is not one who cries in the pulpit but who evokes tears in others." I still believe the proverb, but that day, as I found my voice choked with emotion, I wished I had been more reserved. Still, one who came to the altar that day to receive Christ said that in my somewhat exhibitionist moment, I became believable, at least for her.

Vulnerability opens our audiences like a rose unfolding to light. When the preacher bares his or her soul, that act may bring the leaden-eyed near to see firsthand the wounds that heal. This is the glory of the confessional booth—one man telling another of his sin, the liberation that occurs when two needy souls draw together and say, "Tell me of your humanness and your need; I have a God who can handily fill both."

When intimacy is born between the sermon and the hearer, the shepherd and sheep come to know the glory of that word that we use so often, *communion,* "to be one with." Intimacy takes the last step it can when two who are weakly human merge in confessional understanding.

Comforter and Identity

The sermon and the Spirit are agreed upon one other thing: Identity is a life issue. We spend all of our lives looking for people like ourselves in communities like our own, with doctrines like the ones that we believe. Churchmanship in America is composed of a broad pluralism where many different kinds of churches are divided by only the tiniest shades of differences. Still, we want to go to the churches that are like us. The sermon is unquestionably a key ingredient in this quest for identity. So often potential new members vigorously quiz me before they take the step of membership to find out all the ways we're alike and whether or not they can live with the differences that exist. I always tell them, yet the differences seem minimal.

This harsh business of finding our "likes" troubles me. We nearly all agree that salvation lies in Jesus Christ alone. Yet we seek our "likes" amid the jots and tittles and small-print subpoints of orthodoxy. Fundamentalist churches distrust liturgy. Liturgical churches wonder if fundamentalist churches aren't a bit too "hot." Pentecostals feel that Episcopalians are undersaved, and Episcopalians feel that Pentecostals are oversaved. Pentecostals wonder if Episcopalians will get into heaven, while Episcopalians fully expect Pentecostals to run by it. Gnat straining, we swallow camels.

Most church members do not want the sermon to dwell on Christian differences, but they do want the preacher's sermons to rehearse their oneness as Christians (at least from time to time). How shall this be done? By being sure that homiletics celebrates our identity. Paul said that the "Spirit Himself bears witness with our spirit that we are children of God" (Rom. 8:16 NASB). Such an all-powerful passage is the marker of "like." Jesus prayed in his high priestly prayer that "all of them may be one" (John 17:21), calling for the singularity of identity. When the sermon clearly says, "The Christ in me greets the Christ in you," then identity becomes a powerful bond between the preacher and the congregation and, for that matter, within the congregation.

In the relational force of Spirit-driven preaching, our differences become, at last, underwhelming. The spiritual (or vertical) dimension of church fellowship is always singular—it occurs as individual believers reach outward from the heart toward God. But in the social (or horizontal) dimension, the church reaches out to its community offering the Christ life or counseling or welfare or a haven for the sexually or drug abused. Visser't Hooft wrote in his retirement speech: "A Christianity which has lost its vertical dimension has lost its salt, and is not only insipid in itself, but useless to the world. But a Christianity which would use the vertical dimension as a means of escape from responsibility for . . . the common life of men is a denial of the incarnation . . . manifested in Christ."[7] It is this horizontal calling that welds the identity of the church and remains the definition of what churchmanship is all about. The sermon's vision must remain bifocal, looking both vertically and horizontally.

Further, congregational identity must find its focus in the role model of the preacher. There is one grand congregational assumption: The preacher must be filled with the Spirit of Christ. "It is for love of him that I do not spare myself in preaching him," said Gregory the Great.[8] Richard Baxter long ago rebuked every church that was content to attend the sermons of preachers whose affections were not centered in Christ: "It is a calamity to have many men become preachers who are still not Christians. It is tragic to think they believe they are sanctified merely by their official standing as priests. . . . Such can only worship an unknown God, preach an unknown Christ, and act before an unknown Spirit."[9]

Our Christ identity begins in the spiritual examination of our hearts, for as Socrates said, "The life which is unexamined is not worth living."[10] Out of this examination we recognize our need. Once we are honest enough to admit our need, then we begin to nurture a hunger to be with Christ, to be like Christ, and finally to live in union with Christ.

At the risk of being redundant, let me enlarge on what I stated earlier: The contemplative life of the pastor must grow in a quiet place of prayer. W. H. Auden characterized our age as the "age of anxiety." Gary D. Stratman wrote, "We long for peace: being at home with ourselves, others, and God."[11] Norman Cousins rebuked us all when he wrote, "It is a squinting, sprinting, shoving age . . . silence, already the nation's most critical shortage, is almost a nasty word."[12] The secular noise that chokes our spiritual lives produces nothing. Sermons where God speaks, however, are forged in pastoral isolation. Eliminate all time of isolation, and you will remove the voice of God from the sermon. Pascal said, "All the evils of life have fallen upon us because we will not sit alone, quietly in a room."[13] Here is where the real vertical identity of the shepherd takes place. It must live in the shepherd's heart before the horizontal identity can have meaning. This hurting silence may not be the subject of many sermons, but it is the power behind all sermons.

Comfort and Nurture

"I will lift up mine eyes unto the hills," cried the psalmist (Ps. 121:1 KJV). Why hills? The psalmist is hungry for the nurture of Jehovah. God is nurture for our starving need for meaning, but all of our lives we remain hungry for this nurture.

Nurture and teaching pass close. We have elsewhere dealt with the Holy Spirit as teacher. Yet nurturing is a quality of teaching. Nurturing is learning what the people need or think they need, and then speaking directly to what those needs (actual or supposed) really are. Teaching dispenses a body of instruction. Nurturing is teaching made practical; it dispenses just the right instruction to heal, console, or rebuke. Above all, nurture feeds and therefore stimulates growth, not mere scriptural acumen. I would give my best confidence to such a preacher who understands the difference between mere teaching and nurture.

Nurture's great temptation, however, is to become so didactic in its teaching style as to become drudgery. The late J. Wallace Hamilton of Florida once said, "Clarity, poetry, vitality! Make it clear, make it sing, but above all, make it live!"[14] Nurture cannot be part of our teaching style in the sermon until it is fundamental to our own spiritual growth. Martin Marty claims that his faith was forged by three forces: (1) nurture in the gospel; (2) millions of particulars in which the little pains and glories of life were doing their own emotional instruction; and (3) crisis. These painful, nearly destructive incidents of our lives *do* have their place to draw us along toward a vibrant faith.[15] As I read Marty's testimony, however, I am not at all convinced that these three things are separate categories. They all have

61

to do with nurturing. Life as a teacher nurtures us with pain *and* with simple instruction. Then alone comes the cumulative shaping of personhood.

Conclusion

The ancients divided exhortation and teaching into separate functions of the pulpit. They should not be so widely separated. Teaching is enduring warmth; exhortation is momentary fire. Without the fire, the mind nods off and refuses to be inspired. If we are going to build the life of the disciples, exhortation must marry instruction. When learning weds inspiration, sermons demand with their own authority that sluggish hearts sit up and listen.

Let us pray that the Spirit will keep us company as we keep company with the flock. Then we will not so much preach sermons as *be* sermons.

The Spirit as Power

Waiting upon God is not idleness, but work which beats all other work to one unskilled in it.

Bernard of Clairvaux

Waiting patiently in expectation is the foundation of the spiritual life.

Simone Weil

There really is an awesomeness to the human encounter with the living God. He isn't The Man Upstairs who invites unrepentant chumminess. He is the sovereign Creator, Redeemer, and Sanctifier of all. To come into his presence with a trembling heart is appropriate.

F. Dean Lueking

Power is the preacher's nemesis, the stuff of prophets that we mortals handle with fear. Frankly, most of us would just rather be preachers than prophets. Preachers preach, prophets thunder. Preachers may be accused of haranguing, but popular expectation is generally lower for preachers than for prophets. Preachers write sermons only concerned about the ins and outs of developing their art. Prophets speak for God.

This book is obviously a book for preachers, since prophets don't buy books on preaching. They are not interested in homiletical "how to's," nor do they care about style and preparation. Prophets don't prepare messages. Prophets *are* messages. Prophets major in obedience, integrity, and the demand of God. Having power is not their goal; it is only the supernatural corollary of their preachment. Often the only power preachers are interested in is oratorical power—to enhance, ornament, and drive home their sermons. Prophets have power but seldom search for it, while preachers, it seems, search for it but seldom have it.

There are three actors in the drama of every sermon—the Holy Spirit, the preacher, and the person in the pew.[1] As these actors comprise the drama of worship, they also are the triune agents of power. Preaching cannot be powerful if any of the three are nonparticipants in the work of God.

There are only two ways to have power. The first occurs when our preaching creates a stir so overwhelming that we become secondary to our words. We become observers, as though we were watching something being done through us without our consent. Even when much good is done through such power, we are somehow left afraid of it all, for we control neither its direction nor its outcome. Such power is altruistic: It is totally in the interest of God. This almighty power bypasses our self-importance and leaves us at the mercy of the great ideas that bear us along. We fall into their keeping, freely admitting we are captive to the sermon's ideas and their utter necessity in our lives.

The second kind of power that preachers pursue is only "pro-me," career power—the kind of power that most Wall Street executives want. It is power to be used only for the sake of the wielder. This power has become frighteningly common in this day of big-business gospel. Yet it has only "this-world" clout. It gets things done, not because God has anything to do with it, but because such pastors have learned the furthest reaches of ego force and the advantage of having a good advertising agent.

God's power comes only as the prize of spiritual submission. It comes in response to the need of the preacher to be the instrument of kingdom building. When the preacher prays just before entering the pulpit, "He is offering, and asking. He is *offering* to God the work that he has done on his sermon during the week, the fruit of his toil, the labour of mind and heart. . . . And he is *asking* that the Holy Spirit will do his creative work, will take, bless, and break the word, will confute, convict and convince, will illuminate mind, touch conscience, scatter darkness, bring light."[2] This prayer for the coming of the Spirit is a prayer of giving up the sermon, the bold step of moving from pastoral management to the Spirit's direction.

I recently heard a church growth lecturer say that in order to stimulate church growth, a pastor had to be willing to surrender the one thing that pastors want most, namely, control. God's utter involvement always demands a hands-off posture. This means that the greatest accomplishments of the church will not be our achievements. Neither will all our excellent sermons be fodder for career boasting. The sermons themselves will have a hands-off quality that enables the pastor to challenge and confront so that God may get on with his specific agendas for his world.

A hands-off view of power does not mean that we are unimportant to God. On the contrary, we are all the more important simply because there are very few pastors who are willing to be a channel of any power that does not originate in themselves. The buzzword for this is *surrender*. Surrender rightly implies a relinquishment of all that might be in God's way that prevents the preacher from becoming a channel.

There is agony in being a channel. It means that God has permission to use our lives beyond our hopes for our own best future. Our sense of achievement becomes less important than his ends. The preacher who opts to be used of God will find that when his sermons hurt or rebuke, he himself may become the brunt of congregational retaliation, the object of stinging confrontation. Sermonic power, however, is not possible without such risks.

There are at least two words often translated "power" in the New Testament. One of these words is *exousia*, or authority. This refers to legal right, and means that the preacher who desires to be a bearer of the power of God has a legal right to bear the word. Authority, then, is that right to bear the word that kept the prophets from asking, "May I speak?" Rather, they thundered, "Thus saith the Lord!" What gave them the right to interrupt their hearers—in some cases, kings and queens—demanding their ears? They were the bearers of *exousia,* licensed to speak by their very calling. Every preacher, then, has the right to speak the Word of God. Whether or not he is entitled to the respect of his hearers, his sermon is. He does not have the right to control others or exact from them any duty or allowance for personal favor, but he does have the right to speak. Sometimes the distance between the sermon's right to preach and the congregation's willingness to hear grows great, but an honest "Thus saith the Lord" never has to raise its hand to get permission.

The other New Testament word for power is *dunamis.* This power has to do with word force in the sermon itself. We are talking about sermonic clout. We are *not* talking about psych or hype. We are talking about the explosive (*dunamis*=dynamite) impact with which the sermon accosts and changes the hearer. Just as our authority comes from God, our force must be submitted to him. All of us have seen preachers who once spoke with divine power grow slick with audience manipulation. Such preachers have made sermons mere personal abuse in which God can take no part. Still, genuine power is to be desired, for it speaks in God's stead, to purposes that are beyond us.

Integrity

There is among most evangelicals the false belief that earnestness fathers power. There are those who believe that to desire power urgently is to have power, but integrity provides the matrix of power, not earnestness.

God never champions the lazy mind because the heart is fervent. God's power does not attend a mind in willful microcosm. In my childhood church, we believed that you could lure Pentecost to come again by praying "through" on your knees at the altar. In these long altar sessions, we lifted our tear-stained faces, praying with emotional intensity. We were anxious to have God dump his power on us as a reward for our earnestness. The Spirit of God, however, does not visit us as a result of driven sincerity. Integrity is the invitation to which he responds.

Fifty years ago, books on preaching frequently began with this all-important subject of integrity. The Spirit is defined by one lofty adjective, *holy*. There isn't a more immense modifier than that. To speak of the holy is to speak of the loftiest quality of God. Holy is that remote, other, perfect, and untouchable attribute of God. Holy confesses to no injustice, it is moral oneness with no hint of division.

The word *holy* in every sense resembles the word *integrity*. Integrity refers to that which is utterly integrated, permitting nothing foreign or strange within its definition. Integrity keeps discarding the momentary in favor of the eternal. It continually eliminates the impure in favor of the pure. This Holy Spirit is, in his essence, God, and cannot be lured by anything foreign to the divine nature.

Integrity, it must follow, is the chief quality for the spiritually integrated man or woman who wants to be filled with the power of a holy God. Trustworthiness is the great gift of his holiness. A holy God cannot lie. We may not like what he says to us, but we may be sure it is true. Pulpit integrity means that the preacher, too, is utterly trustworthy. The preacher filled with God's integrated Spirit also speaks an integrated word of knowledge and truth.

Most preachers, I believe, would never intentionally preach what is wrong. It's just hard to ferret out the categories. As Abraham Lincoln said in another context, we must do the right "as God gives us the ability to see the right." Too often we are ill informed on what is right in proclamation. Our preaching remains tied to little issues of right and wrong because our arena of proclamation is small. We live on little planes of small affairs and rarely encounter evil of gigantic dimension.

In my early years as a pastor, most of my instruction regarding right and wrong focused on such things as tobacco, movies, and the like. It was years before I began to get a realistic picture of the immensity of human morality. Pulpits have the obligation to preach the whole

Word until good and evil achieve maximum dimensions. We dare not give our churches the impression that God is obsessed with our naive sense of right and wrong.

Charles Finney argued, "Revivals are hindered when ministers and churches take wrong ground in regard to any question involving human rights. . . . One of the reasons for the low state of religion at the present time, is that many churches have taken the wrong side on the subject of slavery, . . . and have feared to call this abomination by its true name."[3] I shudder to think that there were likely many conservative pastors in Finney's day who never mentioned the great curse of slavery and yet preached fervently against liquor or tobacco. Those preachers failed to integrate the great social wrongs into their small catalogs of morality.

Such preachers were not integrated. In a real sense they had no integrity. What shall we say? Did they lie about the nature of evil? No. Did they tell all the truth? No. Their sin was not that they preached little truths, but that they failed to lift up their eyes upon the wide fields of human bondage. Preaching only the little truths, they allowed evil to control their world. Pastors must study to know all of their world. Those who only read their Bibles often shut themselves into microcosms, never touching the great God who only thrives in macrocosms.

I dare not rail too much on Finney's day. Churches of my own childhood encouraged sinners to lay their liquor on the altar while six million Jews perished in "Christian" Germany. Perhaps Southern fundamentalists in the past also needed honest, holy men to preach integrated world truths. In those days, we often said we felt his Spirit, but now I wonder this: Why would God bring Pentecost to those little moments and not spend himself on the greater suffering that the church was ignoring altogether?

If power does not come from mere desire, then how does it come? Four issues related to power might help answer this question. The first of these is right thinking. There are any number of biblical references about righteousness as the requirement of God. Such frequent allusions should teach us that God will honor the man or woman who wants to do and say the right thing in the right way. Let us "hunger and thirst for righteousness" (Matt. 5:6). This hunger is a picky eater; it will not consume reading and entertainment that champions error or wastes time with obscene preoccupations. Once the mind hungers after what is right, the sermon will also find its appetites in place.

A second wellspring of spiritual power comes from our personal worship, which we have already discussed. Nonetheless, the preacher's character can never be separated from his or her need to meet with Christ in private adoration.

The third aspect of power is the arrangement and coherence of the total worship experience of which preaching is but a part. How arrogant and useless is the sermon that swaggers in self-importance as if it were the entire worship experience. If the various elements of worship are arranged thematically, their speech will be eloquent and, therefore, the Spirit will inhabit all the service and not just the sermon. Music, for instance, as an element of worship, bears great power. Prayers, oral interpretations, dramatic monologues, all join with the sermon to effect worship.

The fourth and final aspect of power is sheer caprice. The Spirit empowers as he will. I have experienced many Sundays when I thought my devotional life, pastoral visiting, and study of Scripture would surely lure the Spirit into our worship, and yet he seemed remote. There were other Sundays when neither my spiritual disciplines nor study had been adequate. Those were the very Sundays that the Spirit descended in power.

I now make no demands on the Spirit because of my periodic disciplines and spasmodic devotional life. I do, however, believe that there is a kind of deferred compensation for discipline in ministry. God, sooner or later, honors the discipline of the faithful. Perhaps not on the Sunday we feel our ministry merits his attention, but ultimately his blessings will come.

The sermon rests on several tiers. The first must be the telling of the saving truth. The Gospels command us to evangelize. William Willimon said that he attended a funeral service for Joe where a rustic Independent churchman was preaching. He spoke confrontational words that were utterly harsh in the face of grief and embarrassment:

> "It's too late for Joe," he screamed. . . . "But it ain't too late for you! People drop dead every day. So why wait? Now is the day for decision. Now is the time to make your life count for something. Give your life to Jesus!"
> It was the worst thing I had ever heard. . . . "I've never heard anything so manipulative, cheap and inappropriate. I would never preach a sermon like that."
> She [my wife] agreed with me that it was tacky, manipulative, callous. "Of course," she added, "the worst part of all is that it was true."[4]

I cannot believe that God's power is going to be attendant upon harsh and unkind sermons. Still, Willimon's point is well made. The great requirement of God is that a sermon must be, above all, true.

One other thing must be said about integrity. Integrity assumes that if we know what is right, we will take care to include no wrong in the mixture. As the cliché says: "Preaching is not a man speaking good, but a good man speaking." Such a preacher pulls the world into a righteous whole and speaks from the middle of it.

What, then, is to be said about certain popular gospel stars and video evangelists? Do they not have great crowds come forward at their invitations? They may, but if they attract people to the person of Christ on the basis of any deception, those who are coming forward in response to their word are not coming totally in response to the Spirit. They may be coming only because of the power of emotional appeal or mass suggestion. God's power knows only one enticement—integrity.

Most of us have a hard time integrating truth of differing natures. The sermon must say primarily one thing; to say two only wars against the integrity of the whole and divides the listener's attention, hiding the sermon's focus. As James Daane observes, "There is at least one basic rule to which any type of sermon structure must yield tribute. *Every sermon must say one thing, and one thing only; and this one thing must be capable of statement in a single sentence.*"[5] If God is one, if all truth is somehow one, then the sermon dare not become diverse in intent or direction of reason.

The God View and the Channel of Power

While I will deal with Scripture and sermon more fully in the next section, let me say here that the Bible *must* be the source of pulpit power. The Bible must be allowed to rise in importance again, and with it the notion that it is the voice of God given to propagate the view of God on all that the church would teach. We must recognize that the Bible has importance and relevance for our day and age. Charles Spurgeon once castigated preachers who neglected the great areas of faith to focus on trivia. These pastors always preached from the Bible but focused on the least important issues of Scripture. Spurgeon complained, "I know a minister whose shoe lachet I am unworthy to unloose, whose preaching is often little better than sacred miniature painting—I might say holy trifling. He is great upon the ten toes of the beast, the four faces of the cherubim, the mystical meaning of badgers' skins, and the typical bearings of the staves of the ark, and the windows of Solomon's temple; but the sins of the businessmen, the temptations of the times, and the needs of the age, he scarcely ever touches upon. Such preaching reminds me of a lion engaged in mouse-hunting."[6]

The Bible passages specifying where the authority of the preacher comes from are the important and authoritative ones. The notion is that God wrote this book; it is "the God-breathed" word (2 Tim. 3:16). Then that word comes into play with divine passion to instruct us with ultimate wisdom that is timeless.

When so much of the Bible is filled with the word *repent,* we can only surmise that God cares how we behave. I used to feel that God was just interested in making us miserable. Starting out as he did with the Ten Commandments, it would seem as though God were the God of the legal: Don't do this or that and you will be perfectly righteous . . . also perfectly miserable. Since the ideas of the legal and the miserable come so closely together, it probably goes without saying that if that was my first impression of Scripture and of God, the preacher should be careful that his preaching does all it can to minimize this attitude in his sermons. This means that he must fill the sermon with the whole Bible, being sure that the breadth of its positive instruction is included when he preaches. The joy, the wisdom, the glad precept, the instruction, the correlation of our destiny, and the continual presence of God—all of these must comprise the sermon.

Our liberated age sees all preaching on sin as binding a sermon to yesteryear. A few, more fundamentally oriented, see sermons on sin as necessary if the church is ever to recover its first-century character. This understanding is largely illusory, however. Any preacher who laments, "Why can't we get the church back to the first century, that pristine time of Christianity's infancy and noble purity?" misunderstands those good old biblical days. When we examine the behavior of Ananias and Sapphira (Acts 5), or the Corinthian congregation, we can begin to see how the good old days really weren't as good as they are made out to be. It must also be said that longing for the good old days, whenever they were, gives the sermon a dyspeptic and unhappy heart. It also makes the preaching only work for the past, since that's when the good old days occurred. Above all, it gives hearers the troubled feeling that they are trapped in an immoral day through no fault of their own, having been born at the wrong time.

Increase Mather was part of the second generation of the Plymouth Colony. A former president of Harvard, he lamented in 1721: "I am now in my eighty-third year, and having been for sixty-five years a preacher of the gospel. . . . The children of New England are, or once were, the children of godly men. . . . Oh, degenerate New England, what are thou come to at this day? How art those sins become common in thee that were once not so much as heard of in this land?"[7] My suspicion is that such sermonizing carries at its heart a grievous dishonesty. First, New England early in Mather's life cannot have been as wonderful as he imagined it to be. We know from history it was, indeed, a violent era in many respects. Second, his hearers could not turn back the clock and live in any other day but the day at hand. We have to live in the now! The late George Burns, the popular elderly comedian, said, "I hate to brag, but I'm very good at it now."[8] Now is here . . . our time. Now is us.

On which sins, then, should the church focus? The church needs to focus on the sins about which it can do something, sins close at hand! This gives the sermon a practical focus. From this standpoint, preaching on the issues of social justice may appear to some a waste of time, not because the issues are unimportant, but because the average worshiper doesn't see exactly what he or she can do to solve them. Preaching on those near sins that the church can do something about is most important, but giving those sins a larger focus can also be helpful.

Earlier I said the sermon should give attention to those issues that really matter, that the preacher should preach on the huge, inhuman sins of race oppression and greed. Apartheid in South Africa might serve as an example here. Such a focus (whether or not the congregation can immediately see a way to deal with apartheid) will wake Christians to care about great evil and live with a civil conscience for all of God's children worldwide. Compared to the inhumanity of apartheid, other, nearer sins will seem small.

In another book I have dealt with two categories of sin; the first I call *kosher sins*. These sins, simply put, are the sins you can get caught at. These are only outward sins on which preaching gains a legal, instant hearing, things such as movies, pornography, drug abuse. These are important issues whose unchecked aggression has bound our culture in misery. Still, they are not generally the sins that comprise the lifestyles of most evangelicals.

Category-two sins I call *mental-attitude sins*. Mental-attitude sins are those sins of the heart—greed, envy, pride, gossip, impure conscience, and so on. While it is harder to get caught at these sins, they do comprise the defeat of Christian growth and spiritual awareness. More than the others, these inner sins excuse themselves and, seldom dealt with, have kept the kingdom of God in tatters.

There is perhaps a third category of sins that are the hardest for sermons to address—the *sins of the church*. The excesses of state religion led to the Reformation and have continued to be a problem with the church in most ages. When the church refuses to speak to its own corruption, there can be no outside chance that God's Spirit will ever be involved in its sermons. The evangelical church in our day needs to speak to a lifestyle of accommodation in which eternal truths may shortly be swallowed up in boutiques and softball leagues. There are so many excesses in the busyness of the suburban church that the church should never run out of relevant sins to address. Not that these sins measure up to genocide, but they do say that the church is pretending a purity of conscience and devoting its sermons to lesser subjects. Vernon Grounds spoke to this kind of sin when he said, "We are sinfully concerned with bigness—with budgets, buses, buildings and baptisms."[9] Let us be sure that our contemporary urge to push a *Fortune* magazine kind of church growth at the expense of every other virtue or value gets addressed in proportion to what it is—sin.

Why preach on sin at all? Isn't it oddly negative in the face of New Age positivism? No doubt it is. Still, without an understanding that there are immutable categories of right and wrong in the world, we stray too far from the wisdom of God. When moral relativism eliminates the word *sin* and then *repentance,* we have no chance of allying ourselves with the Holy Spirit, remembering that he is Triune God. We cannot hope that he who is the inspirer of every great revival of the church will come to us with a newer, swankier theology, comfortably devoid of every idea of sin. He who is unchangeable will not lead the church to repent in one generation and then tell the next that sin is no longer a big concern.

Giving sin its due, I still maintain that preaching must be inherently positive in tone. This is especially true for the pastor's sermons. The evangelist or special speaker may enthrall for short seasons of rebuke and remonstrance, but on a weekly basis, preaching that becomes obsessed with repentance and getting right with God will at last fail. It was Poor Richard who suggested the art of catching flies had more to do with honey than vinegar. We are not out to catch flies, but the sermon must catch and keep people's attention. Sermons that focus on continual negativity and rebuke will fall at last on joyless, empty pews.

Power and the Sermon's Vitality

The sermon and the church need always to remember that neither can live without vitality. So often when the Spirit comes, he brings revival. I don't want to deal with the sermon as the center of revival; still, let's admit that in every awakening, the sermon *and* the preacher were central. The word *revival* has to do with vitality. The biblical word *chayah* gets close. It is a primary Hebrew root that means "to make alive." Life is the center point of all religion. Many of the major denominations are lamenting that they are not showing much life and are losing members at a disturbing rate. The answer has to do with vitality: Neither the church nor the sermon can live without it. The key words that spawn vitality in the fellowship are *inspiration, information, variety,* and *application.* These words, properly under-stood, create sermonic power and never malign the Spirit by asking him to be the partner of boredom.

Inspiration

Inspiration refers to the buoyancy of the spirit that the sermon creates in the listener. Generally, sermons should lift the spirit, not depress it. Occasionally the sermon may need to be direct and cor-rective. At such times it will come across as negative, but for the most part it should be bouyant and uplifting.

Information

Information is the quality of teaching that a sermon bears. The sermon is to instruct, to teach new truth. If the inspiration is drag-ging, or the illustrations aren't selling, or the logic is too heavy, the preacher must be able to change the sermon's direction on his feet. Herein lies a great shortcoming of manuscript preaching. A heavy-footed manuscript can rarely trade its pedantic brogans for ballet slip-pers midcourse. Thus it plods, plods, ever plods, refusing to dance alive the sleepy minds before it.

Variety

Variety is incredibly important. In a day and age when the public attention span is television-commercial long, the sermon must change images at least every two or three minutes or it will begin to lose the attention of the listener. Variety is a great incentive, calling to the sluggish of mind, "Don't doze, you have no idea what's coming next." When the congregation *can* guess what's coming next, the predictable preacher has failed. The Holy Spirit on such Sundays will be at work in somebody else's church.

Application

Application is the final quality without which no sermon can succeed. Application answers the all-important question, "Why should I listen to you? What good will this sermon do me?" All good parents can remember at some time in the past their child saying to them, "Why should I learn algebra?" It is a fair question. "Why, indeed, should anyone attend our sermons?" is also a fair question. Sermons, for instance, that ignore these questions tend to stay embedded in the text. A sermon on sacrifice can get overconcerned about how many goats and bullocks were involved in Aaron's sacrifice on Yom Kippur. The General Motors executive will find such sermon trivia otherworldly. He will demand that the preacher tell him why all these goats are important to him. The preacher who says, "Now, see here, if you don't think you have anything in common with Tiglath-Pileser, you'd better tune in!" Good application may start with a passage in Leviticus, yet leave communicants straining at every step, "Boy, does he have my number this morning!" A little lady once said to me on leaving church, "Who do you preach to when I'm not here?" Hers was the ultimate confirmation that I had spoken and applied what I had said, at least to her.

The sermon's application determines its vitality. Further, our application makes us the partners of God in this matter. Every new sermon bears the footprints of application, and vitality is observed as the listeners cry, "Brothers, what shall we do?" (Acts 2:37). Of course, the Spirit is there. When we work toward vitality in our preparation and he comes again in wind and fire, a rare synergy occurs. There is power from a God who requires the sermon's application to call for change. In this rare convergence of application and decision, the Spirit pays us the highest possible compliment. Earth and heaven are teamed, the liminal and subliminal ordain the pastor as a priest whose sermon suddenly stands between two worlds. Our priestly intermediary pleases heaven and blesses earth.

Power Is the Waiting Factor

Waiting is the grand allurement of the Spirit in preaching. Why waiting? The very word puts us at God's disposal. Waiting suggests that, without God, we do not have the ability to proceed in a meaningful way. Waiting is the evidence that we are not presumptuous. Waiting says our sermon is content to let God be the chief actor, the prime mover, the illumination for the darkness we have not yet fathomed. In waiting, we admit we will not attempt to bear his word before we find out what it is.

The closing words of the Gospel of Luke contain this admonition to the infant church: "Stay in the city until you have been clothed with power!" (Luke 24:49). The opening words in the Book of Acts come from Jesus, who predicts the Holy Spirit with the words, "Do not leave Jerusalem, but wait for the gift my Father promised" (Acts 1:4), and "You will receive power when the Holy Spirit comes" (Acts 1:8). It was the intention of Christ that the church not run out and preach until it knew what to say. This incubation hatched power after ten brief days. The wait was not excessive but long enough to say that impatience makes a wreck of proclaiming the gospel. George Bernarnos, in *Diary of a Country Priest,* warns us that when our sermons precede God, we are like a choir that begins singing whenever it pleases without respect to the downbeat of the master.

We have dealt already (and will again) with several notable revivals. Without doubt, the men or women who spawned them did not find prayer a tedious nuisance. The waiting devoured weeks and sometimes years, but it was never the revivalist who ended the waiting. Rather it was God who, in his time (Gal. 4:4), revealed himself. In such cases, God not only preceded the sermon, but so filled it with himself that his demand broke into the busy affairs of self-occupied mortals unable to resist his coming.

There is a further aspect to waiting and power. It is the willingness to wait while the word is being preached. As I mentioned in the introduction, I am no longer impressed with sermons made short to keep roasts from burning. It is time that preachers confess the sin of pampering restless congregations with speedy sermonettes. I have discovered (through some resistance) that Spirit-driven preaching cannot be monitored with Mickey Mouse watches. I am not advocating that preachers launch into long and tedious orations in an attempt to call the Spirit's power to inhabit the tedium, but preaching that hurries itself into quarter-hour blocks of time for the sake of congregational convenience is too mindful of the clock. No great world-changing preaching made the clock its lord. Sermons that renovate lives place no constraints on the Spirit as he circumcises hearts with new identity. Great revivalists are synchronized with God's purposes, like the vibrations of a tuning fork.

In recent years, we have lengthened the amount of time we give to worship. Our services have been extended from an hour to an hour and fifteen minutes. I have lengthened my sermon format from twenty minutes to twenty-five, but we allow a great deal more time for music and praise in worship. Again, I believe the average person cannot be challenged to suddenly leave a secular lifestyle. The extra minutes, I believe, have provided a little more time for the worshipers to change mind-set, leaving secular preoccupations long enough to consider spiritual needs.

It has taken me a long time to be comfortable with this idea. In the first place, I myself have never enjoyed being detained in drowsy sanctuaries by the drone of monotone logic, but I have experienced many justifiably long sermons, lit with application, to drive home my own needs. Spellbound, I shuddered to blink, afraid I might miss a word. Time only becomes a key concern for us when we feel as though it is being wasted. A fifteen-minute sermon that wastes fifteen minutes is too long. An hour which quickens and gives life can scarcely be enough.

The press wrote of Evan Roberts and his crusade at Loughor: "The vast congregation remained praying and singing until two-thirty in the morning! Shopkeepers are closing early in order to get a place in the chapel, and tin and steel workers throng the place in their working clothes."[10] Any contemporary preacher who tries to keep a congregation till two in the morning will likely find himself lonely in worship, but as long as God authenticates direct sermon application to needy lives, the service must continue while God is doing business.

The phrase "doing business" is key. The sermon must be flexible in this regard. It must be free enough from notes or manuscript to allow the Spirit to move freely to any application he pleases. The sermon that remains rigidly tied to its manuscript or outline will not serve the Spirit. Most people will not tolerate long sermons that are tied more to preparation than the working of God. Nor indeed should they tolerate it.

I am reluctant to exalt the visitation of the Spirit upon the sermon because I fear that in the interest of trying to trump up the Spirit, the pastor may move to a preaching search for the Spirit. This preaching search terribly bothers me. I was recently in a two-hour service in which the preacher abandoned his manuscript and outline—and perhaps his mind. He began to preach in emotive phrases, harsh rebuke, and various haranguing. At the center of his purpose lay the pseudo-hope that the Spirit was just behind the next paragraph of his already too-long sermon. On and on the treatise went, and we tarried till near midnight. We finally went home, forced to admit that we could no longer endure his search for the Spirit. Our hearts were dead; our minds were numb. What was this preacher doing? He was trying to bring the Spirit down as a mood. He was longing after God with earnest intention. Make no mistake about this—our willingness to preach on in search of the Spirit is not the same thing as proceeding in his presence. Our mistaken earnestness should be justly rebuked by those who sit through our long spells of spiritual euphoria in search of a mood that never settles.

There is a final aspect to waiting that must be dealt with here. This is the aspect of waiting as tenure in church leadership. As pastor of the same congregation for more than two decades, I must confess that the waiting from year to year has reminded me of several truths. First of all, growing a church requires a lifetime. Most of my life has now been used in the office of preaching. In this setting, it is not likely that the power of God is going to overcome me in such a fashion that I will never get control again, but I have learned that the Spirit of God comes (some weeks in greater evidence than others) in a continual waxing and waning of power. I know I must live and relate within this seasonal ebb and flow. There are times of evident encounter and times of long waiting when it seems as though God may have forgotten Hebrews 13:5, his promise that he would never leave or forsake me. Still, I know that sooner or later his remoteness will be eclipsed by his presence as he comes again like "latter rains" to refresh his people.

In the ever-cycling season of his presence, I have rarely felt that the church was incendiary with the uncontrollable glory of the Holy Spirit. I must live in the context of my personal walk with the Spirit, marked regularly by my own sins of impatience and personal weakness, and the week-to-week possibilities of God.

Few of the great revivals of history were begun by pastors who had been in the church or area where the revival began. Most people could not say that a revival broke out under the leadership of a pastor they had listened to for twenty years. That being the case, I think it is altogether important that we see the best possibilities of our sermons in another way. The local pastor must learn that his best use by God will be through thoughtful sermons, thoughtfully prepared, and a consistent spiritual life lived openly and devotionally before his people. In this way, he is able to bring a sense of the continuing presence of God to his sermons. To be sure, the pastor will always celebrate the "wow" of the three-day evangelist who can get away with longer sermons, for he has come down to earth "filled with fury, because he knows that his time is short" (Rev. 12:12). For the long haul, the pastor can live with a confirmation of the Spirit of God in his own sermons.

For all it seems to lack, the staying power of the pastor is the best base for a continuing, if less fiery, impact of the Spirit on his people. In the leadership of the church there will be many temptations to quit. As Woody Allen reminds us, "80 percent of success is just showing up."[11] In seasons of conflict and discouragement in the church, the pastor's real victory may be in just staying there while the fellowship is polarized by selfish or mean-spirited souls. Through the ordeal of those "hell-is-other-people" times, a walk with God develops. The Spirit who is our stability through the agony of tenure comes again to inhabit the altar of the faithful pastor.

The best way for the local pastor to think about "having" God's power as an accompaniment to his sermons is to work at his staying power. Noel Coward wrote, "Thousands of people have talent. I might as well congratulate you for having eyes in your head. The one and only thing that counts is: Do you have staying power?"[12] This is the greatest question of leadership in preaching. The sermons we preach will seldom have crusade impact, but they, like leaven, will permeate the congregational loaf, gradually changing the entire community.

Conclusion

The Holy Spirit is *in* us as we preach, but he is also ever coming *to* us. This great paradox lies at the soul of preaching. His *being in us* and *coming to us* are the twin supports upon which God is about to hang the cables of relationship between his world and ours. Without preaching, the bridge does not exist. Without the Spirit, no one could be lured across it. Without preaching and the Spirit working as one, salvation would not exist and God and man would be unacquainted.

Part 2

Word

5

The Bible in Preaching

Preaching is both words and the Word.

Fred B. Craddock

A concert audience does not come to watch a conductor but to hear the music; a church congregation should not come to watch or hear the preacher, but to listen to the Word of God.

Dietrich Bonhoeffer

The only valid starting point for thinking about preaching is thinking about God. A healthy doctrine of preaching springs from a healthy theology, as surely as good fruit comes from a good tree. Begin with an inadequate or feeble doctrine of God's word and the pulpit utterance will be feeble.

Donald Coggan

When the Bible is presented to a new priest of the Anglican communion, it is presented with these words: "Receive the Holy Scriptures. Feed the flock of Christ committed to your charge, guard and defend them in his truth. . . . Receive this Bible as a sign of the authority given you to preach the Word of God. . . . The visible Church of Christ is a congregation of faithful men, in which the pure Word of

God is preached, and the Sacraments are duly administered" (Article 19), and "Holy Scripture containeth all things necessary to salvation" (Article 6).[1]

The Bible is indispensable for getting the God view into our sermons. While I have touched on this before, both in the introduction and chapter 4, I cannot overemphasize the issue. Only this Book can offer our sermons the voice of God. God *is*—this is the great assumption upon which the Bible proceeds. It also is the great assumption on which strong sermons proceed.

Many have claimed that we are now living in the post-Christian era and do not need a great deal of emphasis on the Bible. Decades ago the Bible's wisdom underlay both education and the arts. Now both education and the arts are characterized by a new secularized understanding. In our times, the Bible is under the scrutiny—and, in some cases, all-out attack—of literature specialists, civil rights groups, and radical feminists. It is hard to understand how a culture so founded on Scripture could have been moved so far away by contemporary influences.

The Bible must be the channel of power for the church and the pastor who want the worship and the preaching of the gospel to be subject to the glorious heritage that is their right. Allan Bloom in *The Closing of the American Mind* warns, "Without the great revelations, epics and philosophies as part of our natural vision, there is nothing to see out there, and eventually little left inside. The Bible is not the only means to furnish a mind, but without a book of similar gravity, read with the gravity of the potential believer, it will remain unfurnished."[2]

The Bible must remain central in the American pulpit. It must not be seen as an evangelistic talisman to be held like an amulet of worship. It must be held up as the point of reckoning and the wisdom of God that needs to be learned, and be learned in good time. The Bible is the Word for which the world waits. Society will grow weary of our sermons rather quickly, but the Bible will quicken and rekindle interests. The preacher who ignores the Bible or treats it lightly will likely find not only that crowds will be sparse, but also that there is little interest in sermons made voiceless by avoiding the Bible.

I wanted to introduce this section on the Word with a clear statement on the importance of the Bible in preaching. What are indispensable properties that the Bible gives to the sermon? It seems to me that there are four: feeding, authority, things necessary to salvation, and biblical relevance in the contemporary milieu.

Feeding

Whatever else the Bible does for the sermon, it must provide a sense of feeding. The Word itself furnishes any number of examples of the importance of Scriptures in feeding. Isaiah's servant would "feed his flock like a shepherd" (Isa. 40:11 KJV). Jeremiah dreamed of a day when God would set up pastors who would feed the people (Jer. 23:4 KJV). Jesus' postresurrection command to Peter was, "Feed my sheep" (John 21:16 KJV). Paul instructed the elders of the church to "feed the church of God" (Acts 20:28 KJV). Peter also instructed those who received his letter to do the same (1 Peter 5:2 KJV).

For all the widespread popularity of Christianity in the contemporary West, we must understand as pastors that there is also a widespread ignorance of the Word of God. Most of those who come to church today have no concrete understanding that God has anything to say to them. Further, if they knew that he did, they would have no idea how to find out what he was saying. Leander Keck laments honestly, "The church needs 'the Bible in the preacher,' 'the Bible in the pulpit,' and 'the Bible in the people.'"[3] The Bible, therefore, must precede, infiltrate, and undergird the sermon.

I never leave a single point of my sermons without asking, "Is that all that God has to say about the matter? Are there other Scriptures I might use to buttress and support? Did I use the best, most powerful Scriptures to make the point?" Older pastors of my acquaintance used to speak of "comparing Scripture with Scripture." I believe the idea is worthy. Whatever the primary text from which we speak, we must ask if we have allowed secondary texts to add to the authority and clarity of the chosen text.

As a facet of feeding, I try to understand what the original text has to say. I fully realize that word-study sermons get carried away sometimes in their intent. Many of us have heard well-meaning preachers exhume old word meanings until we were up to our sleepy ears in Aramaic agony. We realize that if Paul had really said everything we are being told he said, Philippians would be the same length as Exodus. Still, it is important to begin to understand a text by understanding the words of that text, and Greek and Hebrew studies of a passage will create amazing insights for the sermon. Robert Roth pointed out in *Story and Reality* that words were used by the Greeks to define their subjects, and the Hebrews used them to describe their subjects.[4] This little insight alone is worth bringing to bear against every passage to be spoken, but the whole idea of feeding is that the preacher is preparing a biblical meal for the flock, without which his church members will be malnourished.

One can only wonder how often church quarrels and struggles are related to a congregation's spiritual famine. Years ago I read a Highland fable that stated a practical truth. The sheep in the Highlands, finding nothing to eat, let their misdirected hunger lead them to the nibbling of each other's wool. They all died of exposure. The Bible is food, and the pastor shepherd is the feeder. No wonder Seward Hiltner has called his view of pastoral care "poimenics," or sheep feeding.

In smaller parishes, a pastor may do this feeding outside the pulpit in his numerous calls to the neighborhood homes. Feeding is done best in small, informal group settings where the pastor's life bears directly and intimately on his flock. In larger parishes, the sermon may be the only chance the pastor has to feed his sheep. If the sermon is poor diet, the parish attitude will soon reflect hunger. The pastor may see this as belligerence when, in reality, it is the cry, "Feed me!"

Authority

In recent years the Bible has been used less frequently in many pulpits. It still makes ritual appearances in such churches, but it is too tangential to intersect with the behavior and beliefs of its people.

Leander Keck observes, "The Bible has seldom been rejected outright. Its place is more like that of an old grandmother who has a room in the house and who appears at meals but who has little real influence on the life of the family."[5] Elizabeth Achtemeier writes, "It is possible . . . to carry on the expected work of a Protestant congregation with no reference to the Bible whatsoever. . . . The preacher's opinions or ethical views can be made replacements for the Word from the Biblical text."[6]

The people who heard Jesus preach were amazed that he "taught as one who had authority, and not as their teachers" (Matt. 7:29). Jesus' sermons depended upon Scripture for their authority. This same scriptural authority must be the force of our sermons.

The Bible, however, should speak in simple authority, uncompounded by the preacher's egoistic need to show how deftly he "fences" with the Scripture. It is always impressive to see a great preacher thrust and parry with the Word as though it were a fencing foil, but showing off with the Word ultimately distracts the mind while the preacher watches his footwork. The preacher should be very careful not to play the authority with the Word. In such deft displays of biblical skill, God rarely gets the spotlight. If the congregation leaves remarking how clever and scholarly the preacher is, it is likely that real authority has been usurped by ego. For this reason, Luther rarely used a Latin word in the pulpit, and he never made a display of his amazing knowledge of Greek and Hebrew.[7]

Charles R. Brown wrote: "The expository sermon is a product of exegesis but not an exhibition of it. It is altogether wise to dig beforehand with your Greek spade and your Hebrew shovel but not to be digging while you are preaching."[8] I am not altogether convinced that every mention of a Greek root should be avoided. There are certain elemental Greek words that might instruct and enlighten a congregation; to hold these words out of their biblical framework might allow for meaningful instruction. Nevertheless, the Bible has very little chance to confront while the preacher is trying to impress.

Perhaps authority comes best when preaching complies to these three kind words: the incarnate Word, the written Word, and the spoken word. This idea says that somehow great preaching couples the prologue of the fourth Gospel to 2 Timothy 4:2 and 3:16. The Word incarnate, the written Word, and the sermonic word can serve as a trinity of authority.

The preacher must never presume that because he reads a text while standing in a holy place that the Word of God is given free course. Presumption is foolhardy. Bernard L. Manning reminds us, "In the twentieth century, it can by no means always be assumed that the sermon emerges from Scripture (as a rose emerges from a bud). Too often, the basis of the sermon is a newspaper article, or a recent publication, or an event of world or local importance. . . . What should have been an illustration (the newspaper article, the recent publication, the event of the previous week) becomes the theme. The Scripture, which should have been the theme, becomes an illustration."[9] Thus authority is replaced by opinion.

The Word of God must remain the center of our authority. Let the sermon be conceived as the setting in which the gem is given the chance to display its natural brilliance. In such a setting, the Bible will create its own value, and the flock will not only be fed, it will find its *raison d'être*. Perhaps the key to authoritative preaching is doing as Micaiah testified: "As surely as the LORD lives, I can tell him only what the LORD tells me" (1 Kings 22:14). Given the art of illustrating, organizing, and proclaiming, this is the safest, shortest way to biblical authority.

Things Necessary to Salvation

The Bible at the center of our preachment does a very practical thing in sermons: It mortars the members of the congregation into a single cause and keeps the church aware of God's intention toward the globe. The contemporary activist church sometimes seeks to find many urgent social causes for the church to preach. The church is, indeed, supposed to stand for something. The social gospel movement put a strong emphasis on good causes. Unfortunately, this mentality diverted the church's preachment away from those things which are necessary to salvation. Most causes are quickly forgotten, and when the cause dies, the activist church may find itself scrambling for a new cause in order to keep its self-respect. Churches that forsake the eternal gospel (Rev. 14:6) to get involved in new social issues as they arise really only participate in the "skirmish of the day."[10]

A few years ago I was commissioned to write an apologetic for the Christian faith as it had come into conflict with Eastern thinking, particularly transcendental meditation. For a couple of years I worked, writing a book to answer the challenge. Unfortunately, shortly after the book came out (and its initial sales were good), the transcendental meditation movement died, as did the reader's need to buy my book. I felt foolish for having devoted two years to the latest skirmish of the day.

Keeping the Bible at the center of our preaching will keep us from trading the best cause for a good cause. The church must never forget that in Jesus' day there were rampant social problems—slavery, polygamy, idolatry, corrupt legislation, political tyrants, and autocratic courts. All of these things did not divert Jesus from laying down the one thing that all ages would have in common, namely, the need for redemption. If the Son of God could be so single of purpose in his sermons, let us beware that we don't make the Bible a handbook for the latest (and sometimes faddish) social cause. Preachers who remember this will maintain a relevance to individual worshipers. Churches that forget this dissipate their strength by running after important causes. Finding their cause replaced by a new urgency, they have nowhere left to go.

Biblical Relevance

Having warned the church against seduction by contemporary causes, I would also sound the warning at the other pole: The church must not use the Bible in fusty ways that leave us talking about how great God was in times past. The Bible is written in present tense, and when the Bible is preached, it must deal with the present day.

H. Grady Davis said that if Jesus had preached his Nazarene sermon today from Isaiah, it might have gone this way: First, he would have talked about Isaiah. Then he would have told what the times were like when Isaiah preached. Then perhaps he would have described how the office of preaching worked in that day. Then he would have talked about the unchangeable nature of God's covenant, and finally he would have asked what Isaiah's words meant to people in Jesus' day.[11] Then there would have been a benediction perhaps, and the gospel would have been left at a comfortable distance in the past.

Unfortunately, our most serious sermons are prone to gather themselves about the God of yesterday. He is, after all, the God who thundered, cleaved the rocks, and divided seas. For all his ancient roarings and universe wrenching, he is without miracles today. The contemporary pulpit must learn to move his thunder into the here and now.

When Jesus closed the Bible and began his Nazarene sermon, his first line was, "Today this scripture is fulfilled in your hearing" (Luke 4:21). The very first word of Jesus' sermon was the word "today," and "today" is still the big word in biblical preaching. The preacher who begins every sermon with that word will be of immense use to God and much pleasure to his hearers.

Contemporary preaching really does work. No matter how the flock comes into church and no matter what questions they are asking, there is only one of real importance: "Is this sermon for me right now?" Their ignorance of Scripture reveals their need. David H. C. Read said, "I learned, when a university chaplain, that the student who asked where Cain got his wife could really be wanting to know whether he should sleep with his girlfriend."[12]

As I earlier indicated, there is much discussion now on whether the gospel should be in the imperative or the indicative. This question is difficult to answer. The word *gospel* means good news, an announcement, indicative truth! Still, the Bible is replete with imperatives, and preaching the whole Bible means that the indicative, here and there, must make use of imperatives—the shoulds, the oughts, and the shalts of the Scriptures.

The preacher must be careful, however, not to promote legalism through the use of his own ersatz imperatives. Having grown up under a highly negative and abusively imperative gospel, I am convinced such authority is not only biblically unsound, it is spiritually harmful. Such bogus imperatives cause those not knowing Scripture to confuse the word of the preacher with the Word of God.

Authority is not the goal of preaching. Nor is our goal to explain the Word of God to the "poor ignorant souls" who attend our pulpit wisdom. Our goal is to make the Word of God into the interpreter of life. We don't preach it to explain it; we preach it so it can explain us. Calvin Coolidge is reported to have said it was not the parts of the Bible he didn't understand that bothered him, it was the parts of the Bible he did understand. The goal of hermeneutics is to allow God to speak through the Bible to interpret our entire value system. It would be better to simply read the Bible with no comments of our own than to allow misguided hermeneutics to obfuscate the sermon's life interpretation. No wonder several apocryphal stories circulate telling of a poor woman who remarked to an astute preacher, "Sir, I completely understand the Bible, and someday I hope to understand your commentaries as well."

A final warning must be sounded: Concordances can subvert relevant preaching in two ways. First, the concordance may provide the preacher with a ready-made outline for a sermon that fits neither the needs of his congregation nor the sermon's intended goal. Second, the concordance may give the preacher ready-made ideas that keep him from digging out the material himself. Every preacher should prepare his own outlines and do all the work that can be done before consulting a concordance. This will keep the sermon uniquely the presentation of each individual herald.

Conclusion

Twice earlier I called for a strong emphasis on the contemplative life of the pastor. Nothing of value is possible in the shallow life. There can be little use in gaining wide understanding from the world of all books if we forbid ourselves a wide understanding of *the* Book. The contemplative life of the pastor must be foundationally tied to his personal affair with the Bible.

Our inner and private affair with Scripture means that we are regularly getting in touch with the center of our selves, which is where we know God. This is not the God of the public sermons, nor the God of community witness, nor the God of congregational meetings. This is the God of the closet, the God of the spiritual center. Without a private affair with the Bible, it is dishonest to talk publicly about its importance. Yes, depth is breadth! The God we discover at the quiet center of our personal devotional life is the spirit of biblical inspiration. He is the one who empowers and speaks, and yearning for him in this fashion will fill our sermons with a subliminal power we had not thought possible. It is not an axiom that quiet time is the guarantee of strong sermons, but the yearning after God which seeks the quiet center is that which fills our sermons with a noticeable hunger. Congregations grow uneasy with pastors who know more about theology than they know about God. A pastor's private affair with the Bible bears unspoken eloquence.

Aloneness in Scripture is the *sine qua non* of all great pulpiteers, but time alone with the Bible is hard to come by. There are a million things that claim the pastor's time, reducing him or her to a professional busybody who is all legs and no heart. Church life offers—nay, demands—a sea of obligations. The good people of the parish *individually* wouldn't dream of taking our private devotional time, but, collectively, they crucify our days with clockish deadlines and "I-hope-I'm-not-interrupting-you's."

Aloneness is more than social detachment. It is a matter of resting the mind from the heavy work of thinking. In my book *The Table of Inwardness*, I describe what I call "kenotic meditation." My view of kenotic meditation is based on Philippians 2:5; it is a matter of emptying the heart of barren busyness. Thus we rid ourselves of the congestion of life, the "roof-brain chatter," that constant stream of thoughts we continually bounce from our inner minds to the top of our craniums. To do anything creative, we have to call this raucous inner noise to silence. In the quietness of self-imposed solitude, surround yourself with good books, articles, and, above all, the open Bible. The creative silence can then stir your womb of loneliness with the fertile quiet of Scripture and cleanse you for the work of public exposition.

94

6

The Word as Art

To interest is the first duty of art.

C. S. Lewis

Starch the bedroom curtains,
Shine the silver tray,
Put on a little make-up—
Here comes the Judgment Day.

David Buttrick

Every conversation I engage in becomes at bottom a meditation, a preparation, a gathering of material for my preaching.
I can no longer listen disinterestedly even to a play in a theater without relating it to my pulpit.

Helmut Thielicke

Preaching first came as a shout of hope. The Messiah had come
at long last! Hell, eternal as it was, had been confronted by life. There
was a brazen serpent, an antidote! The sermon, born as a desperate
reply, was created by two words—the *rhema* (rhetorical word) that
disclosed the *logos* (incarnate word). Both words, however, were silent
without the critical bearer of the news—the preacher.

The desperation of first-century sermons needed neither reason nor art. They bore incendiary and final truths too urgent to fuss with preparation or art. Why outline or exegete or illustrate when the theater was afire? Humankind was perishing and needed neither an artistic word nor a scholarly word. Only a desperate word was needed.

Urgency takes no time for irrelevancies. John the Baptist would not even answer the simple question, "What is your name?" In essence, he said, "My name . . . my name? What matters my name? I am a crying voice—flee from the fire!" (see John 1:22–23). Perhaps the long introductions of guest preachers today points out the change between first-century urgency and the casual propriety of sermons today. Some contemporary sermons are little more than moral speeches that tip their homiletical hats to God. The fearsome trumpets of fiery desperation have settled into chatty liturgy.

Have sermons moved this far from their urgent beginnings? Would the prophets of the Old Testament understand our new, more casual urgency? Would the apostles ever believe that their successors would have time to quote poems—"The Old Violin," "Footprints," or "House by the Side of the Road"?

The Book of Jonah is the tale of a reluctant preacher. His reluctance, slain in the belly of a fish, set him at last to sermonizing. Jonah cried, "Yet forty days, and Nineveh shall be overthrown" (Jonah 3:4 KJV). His whole sermon was reduced to a fiery *eight* words. Surely there was more! Would God prepare a Moby-Dick, Jules Verne extravaganza for something so homiletically unstudied? Surely the clever and imaginative introduction has been lost. Jonah's illustrations, poetry, and exegesis must have been misplaced.

If Jonah's miniature message seems anticlimactic to his Sea World experience, consider how his short message wonderfully cleared the mind. "And God saw their works, that they turned from their evil way; and God repented of the evil that he had said he would do unto them; and he did it not" (Jonah 3:10 KJV).

Peter's Pentecostal sermon, like Jonah's sermon, had dramatic results (Acts 2:40–41). We are told of the instant results of another urgent sermon that occurred a few days later: "But many who heard the message believed, and the number of men grew to about five

96

thousand" (Acts 4:4). Preaching in the New Testament seems to emulate the authoritative style of the Old Testament prophets. Cloaked in otherworldly authority, preaching became the vehicle of evangelism that the early church rode into the arena of the Roman empire. As the common people of Galilee once marveled at Christ's authority in the Sermon on the Mount (Matt. 7:28–29), so the authority of Scripture-based sermons became the word of those men and women who first pressed the strong necessity of the gospel.

A part of the zeal of preaching was the time factor. The apocalyptic age was running out of time, and when time grows short for culture, art collectors go begging. The galleries of Europe, so popular in our day, created little interest during the fiery years of World War II. Desperation always obscures the importance of art. Further, as the amount of time we have to live grows short, we are prone to develop a fervent interest in God. Not only are we more interested in God, we also try to reckon with our finality. John's ancient words, "The kingdom is at hand," in our day cry, "Synchronize your watches— your lives will not survive the night."

No Time to Waste

Following Pentecost, the sermon possessed apocalyptic zeal, demanding immediate action. The sermon was the man, the medium, the message. The product was instant and visible. Evangelistic fire spread, driven by the hot winds of Greek and Aramaic sermons. Congregations sprang up as sermons were preached from province to province. Has that simple zeal been lost? Certainly not!

This zealous declaration is still preached in growing churches. Those who speak more artistic words usually do it in churches already built. Further, those who admire the sermons of the Fosdicks and Maclarens—and they are to be admired—must see that their artistry is unappreciated in the mission slums of the socially dispossessed. Those who are most lost in any culture respond best to sermons not written in paneled libraries, but in the consciences of missionaries. Booth's drums and horns did not sound a trumpet voluntary to call men and women to the queen's chapel, but the guttural "oom-pah-pah" of the cross. "Are you washed in the blood of the Lamb?" was an urgent question that nauseated Anglicans even as it intrigued the poor and downtrodden.

What did Booth say? Who knows? Who cares? What did Whitefield say? Billy Sunday? Finney? Wesley? Mordecai Ham? To be sure, some of their sermons survive, but essentially their preaching was viewed not in some scholarly tradition, but in the tradition of the baptizer of Christ: "O generation of vipers, who hath warned you to flee from the wrath to come? Bring forth therefore fruits worthy of repentance" (Luke 3:7–8 KJV), or Simon Peter, who cried, "Save yourselves from this corrupt generation" (Acts 2:40).

Urgent sermons say one thing. No message is urgent that tries to say two or three things. How, then, is the preacher to build simplicity into his preaching style? Consider these three suggestions. First, when the message is prepared, ask yourself, "What will the people hear me saying once I have preached this sermon?" If there is more than one answer to that question, then the sermon needs to be revitalized and prioritized around a single issue.

Second, in order to be consistent, the dominant theme of the sermon must be concomitant with the pastor's reputation and lifestyle for it to be taken seriously. The pastor who is seen as a congenial relational pastor will risk some misunderstanding if he changes at once to a deep theological sermon on the hiddenness of God. The social-concerns preacher will befuddle his listeners if he suddenly preaches like an evangelist from Georgia. Congregations need time to see their pastors change, and the casual pulpiteer who erupts in thunder will likely bemuse rather than convince.

Third, at the first development, the theme is all-important. When asked how many points a sermon should have, the classic reply is, "At least one!" Fix this simple statement at the top of all preparation and let it coerce the text into relationship with the theme. This practical watchdog line will ensure that the sermon does not chase rabbits.

To be driven home, urgency must be simple. We can all understand the fiery pretext, "Your house is on fire!" We are befuddled by adding a second warning, "Your house is on fire, and you may have cancer!" If we add a third theme such as, "The sky is falling!" we have said too many things, and while each of them may have importance, collectively they cancel out each other.

The Coming of Art

Here and there were men like Jonathan Edwards who combined the best of literary tradition and apocalyptic zeal. In a very real sense, Edwards, the Mathers, and other Puritan preachers supplied a pre-video generation with a cultural center. Their fiery tirades began to resemble the act of a matador—their "amens" were the enthusiastic "olés," where the champion was not really Jehovah but the preacher. A historical theorist writes that Puritans adored sermons. One wonders how, in only a few centuries, sermons could go from "adored" to "endured."

In Massachusetts Bay, two sermons on Sunday and on Wednesday night were barely enough. Five-shilling fines were imposed on the faithful who missed church. Wednesday night sermons were so popular that the court of Massachusetts tried to get all churches in all towns to hold the midweek services on the same night to keep people from running about from town to town to try and get in on all the sermons they could. These were not sermonettes, either. Hourglasses on the pulpit tried each pastor's flagging zeal. If he finished before his hourglass did, it was hard on his reputation. Ultimately, he would be judged an insincere laggard who finished his sermons too quickly to take redemption seriously.

Executions frequently became occasions for sermons. On March 11, 1686, James Morgan was executed in Boston. Joshua Moody and Cotton and Increase Mather all preached to him, and following their sermons, the prisoner preached, warning the righteous to heed his dread example. The four sermons attracted so many spectators that their collective weight cracked the gallery of the church. All four sermons warned that the moral person should beware the decadent lifestyle of the condemned.[1] While, in a way, it seems a kind of dou-

99

ble jeopardy to be executed and to have to listen to three sermons on the same day, these intellectual, zealous preachers were celebrated by sermon lovers throughout New England. In these communities, the meetinghouses became theaters of religious practice.

This theater tendency still remains an aspect of worship. Increasingly the church has welded performance to teaching and exhortation. Soloists, choirs, and ensembles with dramatic lighting all say that the *how* of what we say is as important as the *what.* The increased use of drama in worship—dance, puppets, or pantomime—says the church at worship is a church at performance. The contemporary pastor has become a performer, and his sermon, in a near-dramatic sense, is an artpiece celebrated for its emotional and statistical success (how many respond at altar time). The burden may still be urgent, but it is also entertaining.

In *Moby-Dick,* Herman Melville tells us of Father Mapple's sermon on the Book of Jonah. Listen to Mapple's artistic treatment:

> Then God spake unto the fish; and from the shuddering cold and blackness of the sea, the whale came breeching up towards the warm and pleasant sun, and all the delights of air and earth; and "vomited out Jonah upon the dry land"; when the word of the Lord came a second time; and Jonah, bruised and beaten—his ears like two sea-shells, still multitudinously murmuring of the ocean—Jonah did the Almighty's bidding. And what was that, shipmates? To preach the Truth to the face of Falsehood! That was it!
>
> This, shipmates, this is that other lesson, and woe to the pilot of the living God who slights it. Woe to him whom this world charms from Gospel duty! Woe to him who seeks to pour oil upon the waters when God has brewed them into a gale! Woe to him who seeks to please rather than to appall! Woe to him whose good name is more to him than goodness! Woe to him who, in this world, courts not dishonour! Yea, woe to him who, as the great Pilot Paul has it, while preaching to others is himself a castaway![2]

Perhaps Father Mapple's art can afford to be more obvious than his zeal, for he was preaching in an established church and not delivering urgency but rather a sermon on urgency! One cannot help but

100

notice the difference between what Jonah said and what Father Mapple said he said. The truth is, Jonah's word is the pristine sermon and Father Mapple's is the worship sermon of the church at its liturgical habit.

How Then Shall We Preach?

For years I have felt myself trapped in this quandary. Growing a church caused me to speak of redemption, frequently and earnestly. My sermons have often sounded more zealous than artistic. It was their intent to draw persons to Christ. Is the sermon alone held responsible for building the church? What about the manuals and promotional structures of the church? This question reveals how important the sermon has become, particularly in the megachurches. In fact, it has often taken a backseat to suave promotional programs and attendance campaign gimmickry.

It is probably true that very few of the large churches are being built today from strong, well-prepared sermons. Most pastors are so busy shuttling paperwork from office to office, mandating programs, and refereeing church squabbles that their Sundays come too close together to permit any studied excellence in preaching. Their Saturday night preparation consists of dusting off somebody else's clever sermon outlines for use the next morning.[3]

It may be so, but most pastors would prefer it not to be. Most pastors feel called to do the work of an evangelist and believe that preaching can have both urgency and artistry. For years I have listened via cassette to the sermons of a pastor friend of mine. With great debt to his example, I hear and hunger for both his zeal and creativity in preaching. After he finished a long series on the Passion passage of John's Gospel, I saw the cross in a new light. He succeeded in serving a simple recipe. The burden of his urgency and his knowledge of the Greek New Testament serve well every need of those who attend his church. It puts the demand of preaching in the wrappings of homiletical finesse.

101

Sermons are not only urgent words, they are courage for the dark moments. They shout out across the gloomy waves of depression, "Hang on a little longer." They are fodder for the starving soul. They are great examples of how malnutrition can kill and how defeat is terminal without someone's shouting encouragement. Winston Churchill called England from its rubble and bomb shelters and cried out in simple words for his country's survival. Most historians agree that Churchill talked England back to life. His words shouted courage over the roar of war. This is an excellent picture of the task of the sermon. No wonder John Ruskin described a sermon as "thirty minutes to raise the dead."[4]

Notice that Churchill's "sermons" were not reiterating political doctrine nor talking about political theory. Desperation bypasses doctrine just as it does art. Those who come to churches broken of spirit are not interested in a menu of dogmatics. Dogmatism is authority-sclerosis. It is an incessant filibuster—never mute, always deafening! Talking is easier and louder than thinking. The familiar becomes the creed, the unfamiliar is liberalism and dangerous revisionism. The thinking person off the street may want to ask questions and enter into dialogue, but he finds that trying to ask a question is like shouting into a gale or trying to say the Lord's Prayer at a rock concert.

Unfortunately, the same qualities that give a sermon motive also make it appear quaint or irrelevant; these two words, put together, I usually call "hokey." I have always applauded Huck Finn for preferring to go to hell with Tom Sawyer than to go to heaven with the fundamentalist Miss Watson. After Huck told Miss Watson that he preferred to go to hell, she was angry: "She said it was wicked to say what I said; said she wouldn't say it for the whole world; she was going to live so as to go to the good place. Well, I couldn't see no advantage in going where she was going, so I made up my mind I wouldn't try for it. . . . She said all a body would have to do there was to go around all day long with a harp and sing, forever and ever. So I didn't think much of it."[5]

The logic of the streets is doubly plagued by such images. Why would a robust, open-minded Christ so love an overcorseted, dyspeptic, neurotic Scripture-quoter as Miss Watson? Hell, for all its fiery disadvantages, seems a quieter and kinder place than her heaven.

The Pitfalls of Urgency

The most obvious pitfalls of urgency have to do with meandering, volume, and melodrama.

Meandering

Meandering often accompanies preachers who are so instantly urgent that they never really prepare messages. Their messages hope to make up for their small preparation by their large spontaneity. On the one hand, if you are going to say, "Be saved from hell," isn't it enough to deny the importance of preparation? On the other hand, it doesn't take very long to say, "Be saved from hell!" and so one must fill up the next twenty minutes with something. Usually that something is a redundancy that wanders like the children of Israel around Sinai.

Urgent sermons need to be spontaneous, for mechanical preparation beckons a woodenness that steals from the "here-and-now" urgency. Aimless spontaneity, however, has always been characteristic of fundamentalists and evangelicals in the past and has many adherents today. In this kind of preaching, buckshot patterns replace the rifled aim of disciplined study. Unloaded homiletical "guns" have bent barrels. But meandering urgency doesn't mind, for it often hits something—even if by accident.

The worst feature of meandering urgency is that its spontaneity obscures the ending place. It has made such sterling points here and there in the foray that it grows pleased with the seeking: "I could cut the sermon off now, but if I do, I will never get to the next brilliant thing I might say." What the meandering-urgent preacher hopes to do is find such a brilliant happenstance among his words that he can cut it off at just the right time, then it will seem that the Holy Spirit has indeed led him to conclude his message in power. This, after all, is the confirmation he seeks, but many who attend his wandering logic feel that he has already wandered past three excellent stopping places and that the Holy Spirit wandered out of the church somewhere around noon.

Volume

A second pitfall of urgent preaching is that volume is a substitute for content. We have all laughed at old sermon outlines where preachers pencil in the margin, *"Point weak . . . pound pulpit. Shout."* The principle is more than valid. All preachers rather quickly learn that sound alone will attract attention when the content grows breezy or thin. Urgency tends to get loud anyway, and when you couple loud to meandering, you not only have the children of Israel wandering around Sinai, they are also unnecessarily yakkety.

Melodrama

A third and final pitfall of urgency is melodrama. This is the pitfall that so often goes unnoticed. Unfortunately, the naive preacher and the naive congregation will not notice it since it takes some breadth of worldview to spot this one. Urgency of any sort, and certainly theological urgency, will only seem urgent so long as it does not seem quaint. For instance, my wife and I were recently driving, and we began to sing some of the hymns of desperation that were frequent in churches of our childhood. There were nautical hymns such as, "Throw out the lifeline across the dark waves." There were Elizabethan mind-bogglers such as, "Here I raise mine Ebenezer." There were contemporary second coming, gunslinging choruses such as, "Life was filled with guns and wars and everyone got trampled on the floor. I wish we'd all been ready." As we recalled more and more of these, we began to amuse ourselves. We finally found ourselves laughing. Why?

Was there no truth in such urgent hymns? Of course there was, but their verbiage didn't fit the world, where their urgency suddenly looked more humorous than motivational. Melodrama is easier to

104

spot in someone else's preaching or worship than in our own. While it may be a negative example sometimes, some Hollywood satirizations of the church may help us to see that what they laugh at is obvious to all but ourselves. For as observers, we immediately see what we would not spot in our own worship. Eliminating melodrama requires stern examination. We must spot it before we can correct it. Sometimes just watching our sermons or services on videotape helps us to spot the melodrama so we can clear it out. Leaving it in will cause some to react, "His sermons do not make me face eternal truth, they only reveal how far the church is from the day and age it fails to confront." It is not wrong to say, "Thus saith the Lord," and yet we are more often drawn by the counsel of a friend: "Let us look together at what the Lord saith and how he saith it!"

The Pitfalls of Artistry

The flash of too much artistry makes us look glitzy, affected, and insincere. Unless preaching encounters and changes its hearers in some way, artistry and enchantment cannot be said to have mattered much. The sermon must not be cute, but life-changing. Somerset Maugham said of certain writers, "Their flashy effects distract the mind. They destroy their persuasiveness; you would not believe a man was very intent on ploughing a furrow if he carried a hoop with him and jumped through it at every other step."[6]

Art must be tried at the tribunal of common sense. Did it obscure urgency or enforce it? When the sermon has reasoned, exhorted, pleaded, and pontificated, when it has glittered with art and oozed with intrigue, when it has entered into human hearts and broken secular thralldom—when all of this has been done, the sermon must enter into the judgment of a higher tribunal. If, indeed, our every word is to be judged, one can imagine the last gathering of all sermons—the march of the audiocassettes past the throne. A thousand, thousand sermons, indeed—a multitude that no one can number. Sermons from David Brainerd to Origen, Tertullian to Swaggart, Jack Van Impe to Arius. Which sermons really counted? My guess would

105

be that the significant sermons were the ones where art reinforced zeal without getting in the way.

The God who is the ancient lover of sinners will cry to those sermons at his left hand, "Why did you not serve me? Why did you not love men and women enough to change them? You took their hearts, commanded their attention, but did nothing. Be gone, ye cursed sermons, to Gehenna, be burned to ashes and scattered over chaos, for better sermons would have called chaos to unfold itself."

Art must not, at last, take itself so seriously that it becomes refined and useless in the face of human need. The urgent era of Christian proclamation may not be gone, but most of the world believes it is. While much preaching still retains its urgent style, most people feel such urgency is trumped up.

A new appeal exists for sermons as an art form. The pastor who can prepare, illustrate, and exegete with a great command of words is now celebrated wherever he appears. Harriet Beecher Stowe once referred to the artful preachers of her day as "fox-hunting parsons," largely because their apocalyptic had been tamed with soft living and social club memberships. Whatever becoming artful means, it does not mean that pastors should trade their fire for comfort. The preacher must find a way to communicate saving truth that will cause a professional world to realize that he, too, is a professional. Artistry keeps the contemporary pastor from being too trite while he presents his urgent and biblical worldview.

Declaring Artistically

Art is present to some degree in all of our lives. It is only minimally traceable in some, while it thrives in others. How can we work to cultivate and develop at least some artistry in the sermon?

Seeing the Bible as It Really Is

We have done far too little to let the Bible stand and be celebrated as art in our services. It is time to wake ourselves to the literary glory of that which we handle in such mundane fashion. The ornament of Scripture may be added to the worship hour in the following ways:

Reading it well. When the Scripture is poorly read or hurriedly inserted between anthem and sermon, it suffers. Pastors should practice reading the Bible aloud until its literary glory is orally interpreted for the people.

The Scripture monologue. This is a favorite and artful way to interpret the glory of Scripture. I have memorized some monologues. Others I simply do as readings at special seasons of the year—communions, Advent, Lent, and so on—but all services can maximize the Scriptures as art.

Liturgy and response. Whether done as group reading by the choir, or congregational responses, liturgies and litanies communicate the artistic nature of Scripture.

Scripture anthems and choruses. For many, the only time they ever truly hear Scripture is when it shines through choir anthems or choruses.

Adding Brightness to the Sermon

In addition to artistry, quotations can add both authority and beauty to sermons. I do this in several ways:

Paralleling. I try to think of literary items that parallel the passage from which I'm preaching. Then, where I can, I borrow from the literature to add to the Scripture. Consider this list:

When I preach on:	I can support with literature quotes from:
Ruth and Boaz	Romeo and Juliet
David's faithless son, Absalom	King Lear
Job	J.B.
Adam	Paradise Lost

Cain and Abel	East of Eden
Paul	Great Lion of God
Liberalism	The Closing of the American Mind
Personal struggle	Death of a Salesman
Hell	No Exit

In paralleling, I draw from one source to illustrate a like story or theme in Scripture.

Intersecting. I use brief quotes or illustrations to intersect the theme of the sermon with well-written and authoritative quotes. Intersecting is usually short and most often proverbial in nature, but it adds remarkable authority to the sermon. There are many sources for proverbs: *Bartlett's Familiar Quotations, Poor Richard's Almanac,* Shakespeare, *Don Quixote,* and "The Best of . . ." books.

Contrast illustrating. Contrasting is an old artistic technique. An artist's use of light moves objects to the front of pictures. I can still hear an old art instructor saying, "Dark against light, light against dark: contrast is the drama of art." Illustrations and quotations that provide contrast can move truth to the front of the sermon just as light moves a painted object forward.

Theme	Contrast
Heaviness	Lightness or humor (Remember that comic relief must be used or heaviness will abuse listeners' minds till they cease to listen.)
Grief, pain	Joy, healing, brightness
Rebuke	Affirmation (As heaviness abuses, rebuke indicts. We must be sure that we contrast rebuke with affirmation.)

Illustrating from the arts. Preachers familiar with the arts will give their sermons a sense of culture by using illustrations from operas, theater, cinema, novels, and poetry. This has a great deal more importance than the pastor might know. When pulpits are too discontinuous with the culture, listeners will feel a sense of divorce from the larger world where all must live.

Conclusion

Art and zeal are integral to each other, and both are needed in the sermon. Delete art, and the "pretty" is gone. Delete zeal, and the "heart" is gone. Each sermon should say, "I have decorated to intrigue, but I still urgently declare so that artistry will never be my focus. My focus shall always remain the counsel of God."

7

The Word as Craft

Let chaos storm!
Let cloud shapes swarm!
I wait for form.

Robert Frost

Water, bread and wine are the stuff of baptism and eucharist. Words are the stuff of preaching.

Donald Coggan

Nonetheless, from the very beginning of my life I never doubted that words were my *metier*. There was nothing else I ever wanted to do except use them; no other accomplishment or achievement I ever had the slightest regard for, or desire to emulate. I have always loved words, and still love them, for their own sake. For the power and beauty of them; for the wonderful things that can be done with them.

Malcolm Muggeridge

The Word of the Lord draws the world to church. Still, most people attend our sermons knowing that between themselves and the Word of the Lord are the pastor's words. The pastor's words generally get much more of the sermon time than does the Word of the Lord. Most preachers would say that they believe that the word of the pastor ought to remain little and explanatory, while the Word of the Lord should be in capitals and emphasized. But do their sermons really support this? When we become guilty of reading the Bible quickly, as though it is the small show when compared to the big things that we will say about it, we display our real attitude. How often have I heard a pastor stumble through a passage of Scripture with very few interpretive dynamics, and then cast the Bible aside to emotionalize and wax eloquent. From such sermons, the congregation usually takes home more wax than eloquence.

Why are our words important at all? They may illuminate, explain, expose, extend, and exegete God's Word. They are couriers that serve to guide and direct the minds of our listeners to worthy ends. Our words are the rings and staves that bear the ark of God to Sunday's children. Words nonetheless are critical to human existence. "Like diapered Adam, every baby learns to name the world."[1] We must use words well, for language is "the house of being."[2]

Still, for all of my emphasis on words as sermon craft, this book is not an advocate of manuscript reading. Developing our word power is best done in explicit, written preparations, but speaking extempore can be equally important to building communicative relationships. If the preacher is going to develop his word power, he can best develop it in written phrases, even if his sermon is spoken extempore. These phrases should flow in an easy way that does not call undue attention to their writtenness.

Wordsmithing

A call to preach *the* Word means we dedicate ourselves to understanding the meaning of our words. Clarity is the science of finding exact meanings. Words are the building blocks of sermons. Dan Rather admits that words and their use are so important to him in his business that he took elocution lessons to sharpen both his pronunciation of words and his use of them. Elocution ought to be the lifelong study of every man and woman of God. Every preacher should read the best books on public speaking. Our relationship with words should be fed until we develop a fascination and an extemporaneous proficiency with them. I have several preacher friends who have hand-crafted sermons for so long that their crafting is almost fluent even as they extemporize. Their years of discipline have endeared them to their spellbound congregations.

Words are the tools of our trade, but often they are defiant tools. They seem to have a life of their own. Words are rebels that won't line up on the page. Words hide in dictionaries under spellings we never suspected. They take it too easy mid-sermon when we're strung tight with urgency. They goof off. They snuggle into foam rubbery, churchy clichés rather than firming up their sagging, cellulite theology in fresh exhortation. Words are especially lazy in the mouth of the preacher who refuses to discipline them.

I have learned to be firm with words. When I find a word slouching in comfy sermonizing, I rebuke it and make it stand up straight, and shame it into confrontational persuasion. I hammer lazy words right down into their tube socks with an old thesaurus, and pick up a bright new synonym in leg warmers—a better word, one that's brighter or more to the point. I am constantly searching for synonyms to make my sermons stronger. There is always just the right word to say just the right thing. Why say "cool" when you can say "icy"? Why "icy" when you can say "arctic"? Why "gloomy" if "black" will work? Think of all the familiar words we might trade for preaching power. Did God "speak" from Sinai or did he "thunder"? Did Simon "rebuke" or "excoriate"? Did Jesus "cry" over Jerusalem or was he "seized with grief as a broken lover"?

Picking words that snare the mind is better than choosing words that merely interest. There are words that quit wishing and start bewitching. The sermon can be made to fascinate, even captivate, when we choose verbs with vitriol, nouns that nuke, preppy prepositions, and adjectives with oomph. Words must be made to do honest work as a struggle of the soul. Suzanne Harvey wrote:

113

Every word's dipped in blood
Marinated in sweat, seasoned with doubt . . .
You enshrine a semicolon
Canonize a verb
Beatify some errant phrase
When the seconds stretch like rubber bands
Then snap, boomerang and ricochet
Hurling you back on the blank page

Every sentence is etched in acid
We chisel them from the marrow of our bones.

Good preachers are craftsmen who pick and choose for thrift and beauty's sake. Charisma is a label we pin on some preachers, but we do not usually apply the word to sermons. The word *charisma* means "gift" or "grace." How sad it is that so much extemporaneous sermonizing leaves few literary footprints. The sermon, once spoken, is gone. It is conceived to address, to confront, to heal, but its form is too oral, its endurance short.

To develop artistic phrases and pages is my goal, but since art has a way of usurping substance, I make sure that the "cute" is not allowed sway over content. My rule is "excess within control." Brevity must be conscious of itself. A sermon's literary beauty must not be allowed to primp in the spotlight reserved for power. Brevity means I count my words and make them count.

Wordsmithing will, in time, see our preaching come alive with aggressive adjectives and nifty nouns, but our sermons must never ring with showy craft. Andrew Wyeth is said to have written: "My aim is to escape from the medium with which I work; . . . not to exhibit craft, but rather to submerge it and make it rightfully the handmaiden of beauty, power, and emotional content."[3] The flowery sermon similarly has failed to make words serve and merely set them on exhibit.

Manuscripting sermons is a discipline that aims at both economy and power in word choice. It determines the sharpest, shortest sermon form. In my own preparation, first I craft, then I shorten. I make each part of the sermon as verbally powerful as I can. Then, before

I file it, I look with scrutiny over the manuscript, asking these questions of each individual unit of the sermon:

Is this word necessary to this sentence?
Is this sentence necessary to this paragraph?
Is this paragraph necessary to this page?
Is this page necessary to this sermon?
Is this sermon necessary to the human race?

In all this editing, the final irreducible unit is the word. We sin against communication by allowing words to proliferate. Too many words do not clarify, they obscure. Words, however, are overfrequent now in Christian communication. They fly, firehose fashion, drenching us in Max Headroom monologue. Oh, for a day when communicators, carefully selecting their words, realize what Emily Dickinson did:

> A word is dead
>   When it is said,
>   Some say.
> I say it just
> Begins to live
>   That day.[4]

Words will never live for preachers who don't respect them. A famous dramatist received a package containing a new manuscript. The piece was immature and pretentious. With the poorly written effort was a pushy note that read: "Sir: I would like you to read the enclosed script carefully and advise me on it. I need your answer at once, as I have other irons in the fire." The playwright wrote back: "Remove irons. Insert manuscript."

One would think that evangelicals who are forever talking about the Word of God should ask themselves, "Does *my* word complement *the* Word?" Assuming that preaching is a calling, preachers must choose their words to give reverence to the Caller. Poetry succeeds because it is an economical way to communicate. William

Stafford was once asked when it was that he decided to become a poet. He responded: "Everyone is born a poet—a person discovering the way words sound and work, caring and delighting in words. I just kept on doing what everyone starts out doing. The real question is why did other people stop?"[5] Most pastors, too, at the outset of their calling, consider wordsmithing important. The question is, why did they stop?

Words: The Medium of Sermon as Craft

Producing at least some parts of the sermon in written form can help the preacher toward a mastery of words. Perhaps the first step toward mastery comes with the realization that there are at least two ways to say anything—the more powerful way and the less powerful way. It's all in the words we choose. Every preacher, therefore, must search for words that best communicate the idea. Whenever we finish a sermon, we must go through it sentence by sentence, replacing weak words with those that are robust. Each of the sermon's key words individually must sing.

Skimming for strong synonyms is imperative. For instance, the word *break* is okay. The word *burst* may be better. The word *blast* might be the best choice. I call this search for synonyms the building of sensuous language. Sensuous language is a vocabulary that evokes sensuous responses in the listener. Let me give you some examples:

Abstract	Sensuous
The alarm	The roar of the siren
He criticized them severely	He blistered them with words (Fulton Sheen)
We avoid thinking of death	We disguise death with flowers (Peter Marshall)

Young people enjoy life	Life is sweet on the tongue of youth (Peter Marshall)
The spot where Jesus lay	The cold stone slab (Peter Marshall)
The odors in Jesus' tomb	Strange scents of linen and bandages, and spices, and close air and blood (Peter Marshall)[6]

It is easy to see how sermonic power grows when we create with the proper words. But beware! The artfulness of a word can sometimes dilute the power of simple, direct speech. The phrase, "Christ is humanity's physician" may not have nearly the emotive power as, "Today let's pray for Jim Sanders."

In addition to being sensuous, short synonyms can be used to punctuate with power. Becoming a master of any craft requires the selection of short, effective words. Henry W. Longfellow's poem "Paul Revere's Ride" is an excellent example of this. Barbara Buchman observes that its first verse contains thirty words, twenty-four of which are monosyllables:

> One, if by land, and two, if by sea
> And I on the opposite shore will be,
> Ready to ride and spread the alarm
> Through every Middlesex village and farm.

Simple words are the seeds of greatness, but even they have to be managed. Sometimes the short words that are the most forceful are those words which are the most onomatopoetic (words that sound like what they mean). Consider the suggestive force of words like *spark, stomp, slither, bang, scratch, slick,* and *whack.* Such words are but a syllable to pronounce, though at once visual and descriptive.

The simpler the words, the better the chances your sermon will be heard and understood. I have always had a love affair with the English language, and this infatuation occupies all my spare time: I love acrostics, word jumbles, Espy-grams, and Scrabble. Naturally,

I am drawn to writers who are managers of words. I read Ray Bradbury and Bobbie Ann Mason with relish. For the last few years, every year, I have read all of Shakespeare's plays and sonnets. He, above all, was a manager of words. In *Through the Looking-Glass,* Alice brought up the whole incredible question of how words are to be used and what they mean when they are used:

"When I use a word," Humpty Dumpty said in rather a scornful tone, "it means just what I choose it to mean—neither more nor less."

"The question is," said Alice, "whether you can make words mean different things."

"The question is," said Humpty Dumpty, "which is to be master— that's all."[7]

What marvelous truth to be discovered by an egg!

Ours is an action-oriented day. We are the culture of "what's happening *now.*" The verb world is our world. Verbs are the "show me" words of the language. An abundance of adjectives might have been all right for William Thackery's day, but not for Kurt Vonnegut's. Adjectives dangle. Too many adverbs strangle. In every way, a good contemporary sermon groups around verbs; action flows and the sermon is clear.

The Scriptures are full of strong, clear, short verbs: "Go and make disciples" (Matt. 28:18); "Love one another" (John 13:34); "Thou shalt not . . ." (Exod. 20:2 KJV); "Repent and be baptized" (Acts 2:38). In fact, the entirety of our faith and creed groups around strong verbs—believe, trust, walk, live, and so on.

A balance of words must pervade every quality sermon. Here we leave behind the whole arena of mechanics and enter the subliminal. Editors may tell me, "This works," or "This does not work." I usually reply, "Why doesn't this work?" or "Why does this work?" They often shrug their shoulders and say, "It just works!"

We cannot always tell why we liked or did not like a particular play or book. For some reason, it clicked or it didn't. There is, in good sermons, the proper balance of ornament and argument, suspense and openness, adjective and naked noun, verb and mood. When all words are in proper supply, the imperative balance is there as well. Let's look at Lewis Carroll's Humpty Dumpty again:

"Humpty Dumpty sat on a wall:
Humpty Dumpty had a great fall.
All the King's horses and all the King's men
Couldn't put Humpty Dumpty in his place again."

"That last line is much too long for poetry," [Alice] added.[8]

Alice was right; the last line is too long. Alice could see that, and so can we. In good preaching, nothing sticks out at the end of the last line, nor in the middle. Balance prevails and words rivet themselves to our ears.

Logos Word, *Rhema* Word

I have before alluded to both the *rhema* and the *logos* words. To understand both is utterly essential in preaching. How does the *rhema* word make the *logos* word live? The *rhema* word explains, clarifies, and interprets the ancient Scriptures. What do these words mean in the minds and events of our day? In the next section, I will be discussing word as event, but it is easy to see that when God used words, something happened. Sermons, as much as possible, should be like that!

Preachers are so idea centered that they act as if words were less important than ideas. Ideas may precede words, but words express ideas. Our words do not become mere orations, they individually do their part to set up the congregation for change. The sermon joins with other components of worship, seeking to build a nest where spiritual confrontation may hatch. By its conclusion, the sermon should create a *change matrix* in which individuals find themselves confronting important life issues. This matrix is mostly inward and psychological; it feeds on inner conversation that analyzes, questions, and breaks status quo self-satisfaction. The sermon will only elicit the kind of response it demands.

Am I not speaking in a contradictory fashion? Am I not pitting the skillful use of our words against the idea that sermon manuscripts don't matter? Our words form our entreaty. Carefully selected, they make effective our confrontation by weaving the web of encounter.

Dabar: The Word That Is More Than Word

There is an ancient understanding that words make events—shouting the word "fire" in a theater; the word "war" in Congress; the word "grain" in Somalia. The Hebrew *dabar* holds that a word, spoken out loud, is an event. God speaks, and it is so! Wordsmiths, in the same sense, do not make events; their words, carefully crafted, *are* events.

Does the Bible seem large? To the contrary, the Bible is brevity; it is all word and event bounded together briefly, one small Book, hardly larger than *War and Peace,* smaller than the collected works of Shakespeare. However did God say so much in such a little space? God's thrift of holy words is superseded only by the events of his words.

Dabar! How can one word be an event? "Let there be light" is only one word in the original, and yet this verbal economy is precedent to all of Newtonian theory. When God's Holy Spirit moved upon men of old, they did not rattle on with an easy flow of words. They chose, ever so slowly, and etched their vellum scrolls with event. The Ten Commandments are only ten words in the original. Many of the outstanding biblical events come packaged in word thrift:

"Let us make man in our image."
"Stand still and see the salvation of the Lord."
"Go proclaim liberty."

How simple, how enduring is *dabar:*

"Comfort, comfort ye my people."
"He was wounded for our transgressions."
"How shall we then live?"

120

What economy, what power is *dabar*:

"Thou shalt call his name Jesus."
"Peace, be still."
"Ecce Homo!"
"Maranatha!"

Sins of Sermons

What has happened to this *dabar* principle? Our preaching now is mostly words—eventless, numerous, easy, summertime words. Let us examine the sins of sermons.

Too Many Words

First, sermons have too many words! Søren Kierkegaard has one of his characters affirm that boredom is the root of all evil. How do we make the word come alive? Thinking before writing would help. Paul advises us to "take captive every thought to make it obedient to Christ" (2 Cor. 10:5) before we release it. In another context, Jesus said that we would be responsible for every careless word (Matt. 12:36). That phrase may be above the particular portal of heaven where preachers enter. Alphonsus Liguori tells us of the agreement that Francis de Sales had made: "I have made a pact with my tongue not to speak while my heart is disturbed."[9] Sometimes I feel as though most who preach spin words out of the megabyte mindlessness of a Macintosh mouse. Fewer words, shorter sermons, and even *no* sermons are better than the unbridled verbal geysers that spew from undisturbed minds to undisturbed minds, along that misty passage from comma to coma.

My parents once told me of a hapless bull snake that slithered into the henhouse and swallowed a glass egg. We had used the phony egg to trick our hen by snuggling it among her own authentic fruit. The greedy snake swallowed it, and there it lay lodged in a deadness that not even Alka-Seltzer could quicken. I have listened to some long

121

sermons. It didn't bother me so much that the preacher had laid an "egg," but that the sermonic egg was silicate—dead and undigestable within me.

Undermanaging Our Words

The power of preaching has at least something to do with the slick arrangement and management of words. There is a complex disjunctiveness about life. *Dabar* truth should be simple. E. B. White many years ago predicted a bright future for complexity. Simplicity convinces us that the preacher is, indeed, a manager and an outliner of words.

G. K. Chesterton once dedicated a book to his secretary, claiming that without her help the book would have been written upside down. Chesterton understood that words must be carefully outlined, and those outlines must direct the sense of preaching. Much preaching is poorly done simply because would-be preachers see themselves as all powerful and see words as weak things at their disposal. Complexity flourishes as their words, like naughty children who won't be ruled, rise against them.

Paying Attention to First Line, Last Line

Our first words in life are ever significant. How often mispronounced are words like, "Mama," "Wawa," and so on. Yet our first words signal that we are communicators, at least in embryo, with the world. If the first words of a sermon are well chosen, then the whole sermon is more likely to be an event.

In a random study of several hundred books, it struck me that the authors' careful use of first line and last line generally grouped itself around four ideas. The first-line, last-line usage seemed to focus on either argument, place, person, or mood. My suspicion is that authors who are more choleric tend to deal with circumstances or places. Authors who are more creative or poetic in their writing style tend to focus, as you would expect, on personhood or the establishment of mood.

First line and argument. The first line must cleverly involve and move the listener toward our purpose. The first words of Charles Darwin's *Origin of the Species* read: "When we compare the individuals of the same variety or sub-variety of our older cultivated plants and animals . . ." Darwin started right out on the subject at hand. He is obviously a hard-hitting writer of argument. Whether Christians agree with the outgrowth of evolutionist theory, his is one of several books that gave birth to modern thought. Lines like Darwin's start with an instant demand for interaction. Ah, for sermons whose first lines make such demands.

First line and the issue of place. Tolkien's first ten words in his classic, *The Hobbit,* read: "In a hole in the ground there lived a hobbit." In spite of his poetic, creative style, Tolkien began with the matter-of-fact assumption of place. The same assessment might be made of the first six words of *Don Quixote:* "In a village of La Mancha . . ." The first five words of Garrison Keillor's best-seller read: "The town of Lake Wobegon . . ." Isak Dinesen's *Out of Africa* begins: "I had a farm in Africa, at the foot of the Ngong Hills."

Place is a cry of identity in the sermon. When we hear the name of a person in a sermon, our first reaction is, "I know him or her," or, "I don't." When we hear the name of a place, we think, "I've been there," or, "I haven't," or, "I know of that place," or, "I don't." Place is therefore an automatic claimant of sermonic interest.

First line and the meeting of persons. Meeting others brings interest to our lives. In our first sermon words, a sense of relationship is established. Frederick Buechner begins his novel *Godric* simply: "Five friends I had, and two of them snakes." Herman Melville begins *Moby-Dick* with three words: "Call me Ishmael." In the opening sentences of *Dr. Zhivago,* the text reads: "'Who is being buried?'— 'Zhivago' . . ." People are ideal launching platforms for sermons, too.

In every sermon, I welcome "mini-biographies," the excerpted lives of people with apt description of their manners of thought or speech. To hear of people described quickens the value of illustration. If novelists begin a story with a person, the first lines of a sermon may also profit from the technique. I still remember hearing a preacher describe Jezebel of Israel, and while I found her contemptible, I also found her fascinating.

First line and mood. Moods, well described, are also a hook for interest. The first three words of M. Scott Peck's great work, *The Road Less Traveled,* read: "Life is difficult." Virginia Stem Owens sets the mood in *And the Trees Clap Their Hands* with the words: "My companion and I sit by the window in a coffee shop, watching snowflakes spin and drift to the solid sidewalk. . . ." Sermons that cast a mood in the first lines may be able to weave them also in the last critical lines as well.

First line and poetic beginnings. I generally opt for poetic beginnings in my own books. I began *The Singer* with: "For most who live Hell is never knowing who they are." It is sometimes right to begin the sermon with singing lest the possibility of song be lost. W. E. Sangster suggested that introductory words should be brief, interesting, and arresting. To illustrate the principle, he cited two practical and brief introductions: On June 2, 1918, after four years of war, J. N. Figgis, before Cambridge University, in an atmosphere of national fear, began: "'The Lord sitteth upon the flood; yea, the Lord sitteth King for ever' (Ps. 29:10, K.J.V.), and he began at once with one tense question: *'Does he? Does he?'"*[10]

Sparhawk Jones at Princeton University Chapel announced his text: "'Is thy servant a dog, that he should do this thing?' (II Kings 8:13, K.J.V.). After a moment's pause, he began crisply: 'Dog or no dog, he did it!'"[11]

Sangster, who was big on captivating beginnings, nonetheless felt they should always be brief:

> Years ago I used to pass on my way to my church a wee house with an enormous porch. I see it in my mind's eye as I write. Great Corinthian pillars complete with acanthus leaves supported a baroque portico which would have given shelter from the rain for half a platoon of soldiers. On the other side of this enormous porch was something like the cheapest kind of council house. I always smiled as I went by. It reminded me of . . . certain sermons I have heard.[12]

Preachers, like authors, must choose their words so that others can't second-guess them. Whatever our first words are, they must avoid the predictable. Consider this refreshing beginning of *Huckleberry Finn*: "You don't know about me, without you have read a book by the name of 'The Adventures of Tom Sawyer,' but that ain't no matter. The book was made by Mr. Mark Twain, and he told the truth, mainly. There was things which he stretched, but mainly he told the truth."

Conclusion

Here and there, I have found a *dabar* preacher. Enchanted, I have heard his word-events and been stopped by a mind whose words were sunny windows on a broad world. Into such a wide world Jesus came, and while he told us to go into all the world to make disciples, it's okay if we look around as we go. Seeing widely packs our words with light, and inner light of some sort is surely the sermon's conscience. To see with such an eye makes the preacher a force of one in a world where many eyes, glazed by television, have seen only the edge of light and fallen asleep without wonder.

8

The Word as Reputation

Take our minds, and think through them.
Take our lips, and speak through them.
Take our hearts, and set them on fire with love for thee.
What we know not, teach us.
What we have not, give us.
What we are not, make us.
For Jesus Christ's sake.

Donald Coggan

To stand and drone out a sermon in a kind of articulate snoring to people who are somewhat between awake and asleep must be wretched work.

Charles Haddon Spurgeon

If I use a word or phrase you do not understand, you are to stop me.

John Wesley

Everybody has a reputation, be it good or bad. Preachers need a "good report" from outsiders (1 Tim. 3:7). Most preachers would like their preaching to be a part of the reason for their good report. We are not content to have a "good Joe" reputation that is merely kind, charitable, or relational. Our sermon word is also important to our reputation. Preachers want to be known as boom-lowerers, hot rods, or powerhouses. For all the charm of the word *pastor,* come Sunday morning we would rather be viewed as an oratorical force to be reckoned with than as just a nice little pastor. We want to move our community to come and hear us preach. Our sermons should serve our reputation in three areas—mobility, authenticity, and incarnation.

Mobility

Barbara Tuchman says that over her typewriter she has a sign that reads in big, bold letters: "Will the reader turn the page?"[1] The issue behind her concern is mobility. When we finish a sermon, can we honestly say that our listeners were propelled along by brisk logic, or does our preachment mire down and lose its way?

The difference between a pond and a stream is mobility. There is always the feeling that a stream is going somewhere, and therefore it is more interesting. Sermons are often ponds, too undisciplined to flow, too shallow to be buoyant. They are altogether out of sync with our highly mobile times.

Static versus Movement

In the closing years of the twentieth century, static is out, movement is in. We have become accustomed to new cinema forms that bombard us with visual images driving the plot pell-mell before it. If cinema interest sags, the best producers throw in visual snags to draw theatergoers out of their popcorn sacks and back to renewed attention.

In such a day, churchgoers, like theater patrons, will not tolerate a stodgy form. The sermon must move. It is difficult to speak of all the things that make for mobility, but as a general rule, simplicity sells. What are the elements and enemies of movement in the sermon?

Enemies of Mobility

Predictability. In extemporaneous sermons, there are three enemies of mobility. The first is predictability. The familiar does not intrigue us, only the unique. As the proverb says: Familiarity breeds contempt. All preachers recognize that there is security in that which is comfortable. To provide comfort, preaching frequently grows safe with clichés. Yet the same familiarity that protects is also a killer. Certain old poems warm us with remembrance but pack in the same old schmaltz that snuggles congregations into slouchy, comfortable, time-worn rhetoric.

Ostentatious style. As predictability is the enemy of mobility in sermons, so is any language that calls attention to itself. Alliteration usually jars a listener to a sudden stop. Preachers often alliterate their outlines with something like "Sin, Salvation, and Security," or, "The Man, the Medium, and the Message." Any time the focus leaves the subject of the sermon and becomes centered on the cleverness of the words themselves, movement falters. As tools, words are not to be admired but to construct a framework for the true subject.

The terminology trap. On the research end of sermons, there is a tendency to fall into the terminology trap. Another fault of preachers whose degrees are still set with new ink is that they believe hoity-toity rhetoric is the way of the cross. It is, of course, but only for those who listen. Edwin Newman in *Strictly Speaking* further defines the terminology trap that preachers often fall into. Newman suggests that had Lincoln fallen into this trap, he would have said: "God must have loved the people of lower and middle socio-economic status, because he made such a multiplicity of them," rather than, "God must love the common people because he made so many of them."[2] Pumping the sermon full of elitist words always slows the sermon's movement.

Questions the Mobile Sermon Must Answer

Is this professional? Professionalism is the hardest of all the issues to deal with. A great deal of experience and a wide awareness is required to answer this one. A sermon is too complex if it brings up more questions than it can handle. To prohibit this complexity, the preacher should keep the tenets few and ask all along the preparation: "What are the antecedents of my argument? Do I appear trustworthy because of my grasp of the subject? Can my professionalism be measured by the kinds of sources I quote?" All quotations must have some general respect before the sermon can earn any. In sermonic speaking, it would be better to quote Billy Graham than Sun Myung Moon. When speaking of theology, it would be better to cite Martin Marty than Joseph Smith.

Does it move without distraction? An answer to the question of mobility comes by asking, "Does the sermon cohere and does it move toward its conclusion free of hang-ups?" Perhaps it would be more honest to ask, "Does the sermon really know where it's going?" It is generally good to write the sermon theme into one clear sentence before the sermon preparation ever begins. This single-theme sentence then becomes the director of both preparation and delivery: "Luther insisted on finding the *Sinnmitte,* the heart of the text. That heart, that *Kern,* or kernel is to save the preacher from getting lost in details. . . . The main point of a sermon is to be so clear in the preacher's mind that it controls everything that is said."[3]

Amateurs stray. Professional preachers do not. Remember little Mary's essay on pigs?

A pig is a funny animal, but it has some uses [the uses are not mentioned]. Our dog don't like pigs—our dog's name is Nero. Our teacher read a piece one day about a wicked man called Nero. My Daddy is a good man. Men are very useful. Men are different than women and my Mom ain't like my Daddy. My Mom says that a ring around the sun means that a storm is coming. And that is all I know about pigs.[4]

Little Mary may be excused for her digressions, but no one would say that her research is professional. Yet, sadly, I have sat through sermons that wandered from Dan to Beersheba and never told me the subject of the message.

Does the sermon avoid colloquialisms and clichés? Bloopers are a special danger in the extempore style of preaching. Unfortunately, bloopers are the province of us all. As a speaker and a writer, I am aware that lurking behind every paragraph of my sermon is the possibility I will get my "tang all tonguelled up." In preaching, even bloopers are a lesser evil than colloquialisms.

We must all be on the lookout for colloquialisms. While they may comprise the fabric of our warm and wonderful way of life, sanctified colloquialisms are just as distracting as the more jivey, secular ones. Evangelicals as such have a religious vocabulary that characterizes their way of life. We must be most careful not to let this lingo riddle our sermons with religious clichés. These clichés have a tendency to become exaggerated as we write and speak. Things usually tend to be more "glorious" than necessary in evangelical sermons. Many who accept Christ have "victorious experiences." Church budgets tend to be as "fantastic" as revivals are "glorious." Choir specials are "thrilling," and prayer meetings are all-too-often filled with "Hallelujah."

I once heard of a busload of evangelists on tour who praised the Lord all the way to the Grand Canyon and suddenly, upon seeing the world wonder, they were out of adjectives, having squandered all their great words in little ways. Well, "bless God and the Lamb," we know we had better be careful or we could really get "in the flesh" and "quench the Spirit" in our preaching. Maybe you've noticed that when some preachers are "livin' for Jesus" and "prayin' through" and "waitin' for the rapture," it gets hard to talk normal. How does one preach on being "saved, sealed, and sanctified" and bar those words from our sermons?

Religious clichés are not the only clichés that infect sermons. As preachers, we need to avoid those which the media foist upon society. Media clichés and colloquialisms are as wooden as any other kind. Their prefab phrases are stilted and they squelch originality. Terms like "hope of détente," "an uneasy truce," "the emergence of the Third World," and "fiscal policy" do not lubricate mobility.

Being Mobile, Being Human

To be most mobile is to be human in the sermon. Preachers, like poets or novelists, must know the joy and pain of life. Sermons that emanate from empathy can speak to those who live in pain. John Killinger says it well: "We must love people and love God's vision of the community. Then we can preach."[5] Mobility happens when real, live people preach to real, live people. The church as a community is waiting for a word of love from the pulpit. Our listeners are persons who hurt and laugh and feel, and they relate to those same human qualities in their preacher. I'm on the side of the Tin Woodman in his debate with the Scarecrow in *The Wizard of Oz*. The Scarecrow, desiring brains, asks the Tin Woodman, "Have you any brains?" The Tin Woodman answers, "No my head is quite empty, . . . but once I had brains, and a heart also; so, having tried them both, I should much rather have a heart."[6]

The sermon's mobility flows best when the sermon directs its remarks to the common mind rather than the erudite. Martin Luther understood: "I don't think of Dr. Pomeranium, Jonas or Philip in my sermon. They know more about it than I do. So I don't preach to them. I just preach to Hansie or Betsy."[7] If Hansie and Betsy understand our words, we will likely preach sermons that move. If not, then we shall be guilty of what Charles Spurgeon called "giraffe" mentality: "To the problem of preaching over people's heads, Spurgeon wittily commented: 'Christ said, "Feed my sheep." . . . Some preachers, . . . have read the text, "Feed my giraffes."'"[8] Such high feeding will mire the sermon in question marks, and mobility is left like a tortoise in a marathon.

Authenticity

Personal Authenticity

Openness does not have to do with reputation. Openness *is* reputation. Openness is a facet of general reputation that adheres to the preacher. Throughout his community and parish, the preacher should be well respected and generally seen as open. The moral accusations against television evangelists in the 1980s prove that people will not hear a preacher say anything until they respect him as open and honest.

As people listen to sermons, they are in continual dialogue with themselves. Their minds are each split in two, and the two lobes of their argument converse:

"Does the man speak the truth?"
"Did that illustration really happen to him as he told it?"
"Oops, he gave the wrong credit on that quote."

Most people are willing to bend and forgive honest errors or improper footnotes, but they will not forgive blatant dishonesty or vaudeville illustrations where the immensity of the style overtakes the simplicity of the message.

All we who preach are tempted to use the best parts of other great sermons we have heard. With sermon cassettes available everywhere, it is easy to capture another's originality and label it as our own. Using other's materials is not wrong, properly credited, but all rhetorical thievery, unacknowledged, is reprehensible.

A Midwest preacher recently plagiarized one of America's popular radio preachers. He preached an entire sermon he had heard on radio. In this particular sermon, the radio preacher mentioned a dream that he had had, and so the plagiarizing pastor also mentioned the dream as though it were his own. As ill luck would have it, the original sermon was repeated the next day on the radio. Some in the plagiarist's congregation said, "Can you believe it, that radio preacher copied one of our pastor's fine sermons?" But most saw immediately who had copied whom. The next week, the deacons wisely asked the shamefaced pastor to confess his plagiarism. The credibility of that pastor's future sermons was wounded. His listeners, from week to week, will always wonder if he has originated every subsequent good idea or if he is listening to the radio again.

133

Another pastor was caught preaching (nearly word for word) someone else's sermons. He was not fired, but his public embarrassment was costly to his image.

Why all this fuss? Integrity is a hard-bought reputation. Without it, we cannot convince the waiting world that we are to be trusted when we tell them that this is what they ought or ought not to do. Authenticity alone deserves the title of "the chief ingredient of lasting motivation." In this sense, the motivator's task becomes teleological—the task of finishing men and women as he believes that he himself would like to be finished.

According Dignity to All

The initial rapport preachers establish with their listeners must not overinfluence. Delivering what we promise in our sermons is as important as any other aspect of reputation. Vance Packard reminds us, "A good profession will not represent itself as able to render services outside its demonstrable competence."[9]

Applying too much pressure is an evidence that we are either unaware of others' individual and personal worth or that we have no respect for them. It is easy in haughty preaching to look down on people whose experiences and pilgrimages do not measure up to our overstated sermon ideals. When we fail to be concerned about people because we see them as significantly beneath our level of achievement, we depersonalize them. We may in fact motivate them in this depersonalized state, but in such instances we become manipulators and are no longer ministers. Harry Levinson calls this *The Great Jackass Fallacy,* and says that we often strip people of dignity as though we are "dealing with jackasses."[10] How often is church promotion handled this way? To pastors guilty of these carrot-and-stick tactics, everything is permissible—Shetland ponies, Holy Land junkets, and cash giveaways. Such crass dehumanization puts us in the queue with the commonest of hucksters. At this point in our discussion we need to turn our attention to the proper understanding of the nature of authenticity in the influencer himself.

Recognizing Who We Are Psychologically

Among all communicators, credibility comes first. This is especially true in the pastor. To find the most honest course as a motivator, the pastor should take stock of himself and his values. Exactly
what motivates a man to become a pastor, a motivator himself? Psy-
chiatrists are commonly and unfairly accused of being disturbed men
who picked a profession that promised them the key to their troubled souls. Why do most ministers pick the ministry? While some
allowances must be made for the call of God, a majority of ministers
have mother-dominated childhoods replete with psychological needs
which they may attempt to fill in spiritual ways.

The pastor-motivator is often tempted to confuse his images of the
kingdom with those of his own personal career. Is he, for instance,
starting a bus program for Jesus or for his own self-importance among
his peers? When he loses the distinction between the two, he is apt to
become a manipulator. If he is successful at manipulating others, he
will find it increasingly more difficult to arrest this approach and return
to his original premises. After all, when you are manipulating, where
do you stop? For the pastor, the key is not to govern his motivation by
that which is socially undesirable, but by that which is spiritually undesirable. There is nothing wrong with motivation, as long as the ends to
which we motivate are squarely in the interest of the persons we are
motivating. The failure to take motivation seriously will leave the pastor a namby-pamby creature whose organizational goals are diffused
and whose sermons are confused. People really want to be motivated;
they seek motivation, but they resent being used.

Jesse Nirenberg says in an excellent book that the best kinds of
motivation are purely rational. Motivational communication is always
dialogical. He cautions us to remember that good dialogue is marked
by rapt attention on the part of both parties.[11]

Not Wasting the Listener's Time

Holding people's attention means that we must not take more time
than a subject is worth. How much cumulative time do I waste on

135

Sunday mornings when I have not worked hard to say something? If, in my sermon, I waste thirty minutes of time for two thousand people, I have blown one thousand hours of human attention. That's an astounding six weeks of a single life. Authenticity demands an impeccable stewardship in life. If I, through sloppy preparation and an undisciplined study life, can waste such vast amounts of time, I am not worthy of the label "honest."

Replacing Sermonic Threat with Affirmation

The sermon needs to ask three questions of its listeners.

Does the word scold or exalt personhood? Affirmation is a property of authenticity. The pastor who pontificates or scolds his listeners for the purpose of exalting himself has lost track of integrity. Sound prophetic rebuke has its place within the sermon, but if it does not cause the preacher pain as he preaches, he has no integrity. The spirit of affirmation is the crown of authentic preaching. The congregation is loved by God and worthy for that reason (if for no other) to be addressed in love.

Does this sermon thank or take for granted? Remember, our listeners have come to hear us of their own accord. Let us be sure we communicate our thanks for this gift to us. Robert Townsend reminds us that thanks is a neglected form of audible compensation.[12] Ray C. Hackman listed praise as the second-most valuable incentive in the motivation field.[13]

If this holds true in industry, surely "thanks power" can become a potent form of motivation in the church. Many times on a Sunday someone remarks that the church has not appreciated them. "Thanks" is a term of validation. The person who has been thanked feels both valued and loved. Harry Levinson reminds us: "People experience loss of love when the organization changes its ways of treating its people so that they feel less valued."[14] Perhaps it should be noted that false praise clearly marks the sycophants, and the insincere "gusher" will soon be discovered. His flattery will not support him for long in his attempt to motivate. Praising people must not be void of authenticity.

Does this sermon rebuke, or threaten? Rebuke can occasionally be justified—threats never! Finally, threat as a motivation was kept till last, probably because it is the most distasteful. It can be a legitimate form of motivation only if the threat is real and the one being motivated is in some real danger. The evangelist or pastor who cries out, "If you do not come to visitation, the blood of many lost people will be on your hands," has most likely neither a love for God nor his people. Threat on a consistent basis is usually ineffectual. It is like the boy who cried "Wolf!" so frequently that it became no motivation at all.

Kenneth Blanchard was asked in *The One-Minute Manager* how he motivated others, and he replied that he caught somebody doing something right and made a federal case out of it.[15] The wise pulpiteer must remember that this is a most wholesome alternative to threat in preaching.

Incarnation

As Jesus was an incarnation of the Father, even so we are to be incarnations of Jesus. This is true in terms of the indwelling Spirit who is to speak from our lives and through our lives. I want to consider the word *incarnation* from another level, when, as Marshall McLuhan suggests, the medium is the message.

Medium and Message

Marshall McLuhan entitled his dramatic book *The Medium Is the Message.* I have often felt that nothing could be truer in the sermon. Churches do not hear messages; they hear only the man or woman who speaks the message. Before any preacher stands to speak, we have already formed an opinion about how effective we think his or her message will be. Sometimes just the appearance of the preacher will tell us how good the sermon will be, and our supposed impression is very often right.

It struck me one day that the world's greatest thinkers did not preserve their ideas in books, but left followers who, like themselves, were also unpublished. In spite of this, their truths survive. How true this is of Jesus. He never published books, but returned to heaven with his greatest words secure in the hearts of his disciples. For some years after that time, Jesus' teachings remained unprinted.

A fanatic has been defined as a person who "can't change his mind and won't change the subject." Perhaps preaching in its inception appeared to be a hang-up. "These men who have caused trouble all over the world have now come here," said the critics of Paul and the apostles (Acts 17:6). Some of the most effective communicators of the gospel did not attempt to speak on a wide range of subjects.

How does this square with another subtheme of this book—namely, that preachers ought to be educated widely and interested in their world? This tension between narrowness and reading broadly must be resolved in this way: Preachers must not allow their need for wide understanding to blunt the focus with which they preach the simplicity of the gospel. In the pastor there must be a hunger to avoid naiveté (a contentment with little understanding) and, at the same time, to realize that the greatest truths of every culture are so simple that they bind the mighty with simple strings.

How will the double bind serve? On the one hand, the pastor who has encountered the immense amount of truth that exists in his world will not judge a priori those who do not know or celebrate Christian truth. On the other hand, his confidence is that to know Jesus is to know the only truth that can redeem man. Donald Coggan wrote about the great need of the preacher to be sold on incarnational sermons: "Again and again such a preacher will find himself returning to the Person of Christ, incarnate, crucified, risen, glorified, present among us, coming to us."[16]

We are to be forever locked in this inner struggle with ourselves. Long ago, Elton Trueblood called the Christian intellectual the "new man for our time." He understood that nurturing the mind undermines the cozy nest of naiveté out of which preaching grows sure of itself. There is more truth than error in the cliché, "It's hard to be as naive as we would like." Our lives as pastors, however, need growing intellects as well as fervent words. Growing in heart and mind means that our preaching will be a continual Gethsemane, where we ask as

Jesus asked, "Father, if it be possible, let this cup pass from me: nevertheless not as I will . . ." (Matt. 26:39 KJV). Great preachers are never those who have resolved every doubt or inner conflict, but those who remain honest in their intellectual conflicts and continue to grow as they preach with fervor such truths as they know to be redeeming.

Conclusion

In conclusion, the sermon must serve these three areas of reputation: mobility, authenticity, and incarnation. Mobility comes from crafting the exposition carefully. Authenticity comes from a determination to let the preacher's humanity be mingled with the sermon's high purpose. Incarnation speaks of the indwelling Christ. Christ will not indwell the sermon unless he has taken up an unbroken residence in the preacher.

Where these three words describe the sermon, the kingdom of God will be found. The church will both evangelize and equip. Instruction will be mingled with exhortation, and commitment with worship.

Part 3

Story

9

The Sermon as Story

Tell me the same old story
When you have cause to fear
That this world's empty glory
Is costing me too dear.

Tell me the story, always,
If you would really be,
In any time of trouble,
A comforter to me.

A. Catherine Hankey

It also became clear to me that if I desired to communicate anything on this point, it would first of all be necessary to give my exposition an indirect form.

Søren Kierkegaard

"And that's the whole poem," he said. "Do you like, Piglet?"
"All except the shillings," said Piglet. "I don't think they ought to be there."

"They wanted to come in after the pounds," explained Pooh, "so I let them. It is the best way to write poetry, letting things come."

"Oh, I didn't know," said Piglet.

A. A. Milne

Preaching is, in every sense, a grand bridge with one pier in the distant, holy *then* and the other in the not-so-sacred *now*. Preaching roots around in the age of cuneiform calendars to bring meaning to those who measure life by glitzy quartz chronometers. What glory is preaching? Why should anyone care about old sheiks and bigamists hungering for a word from Yahweh as they turned from Baals and ziggurats to find meaning in the blistering winds of Horeb? We who preach reach back to their nomadic existentialism to find what we must say to the needy nomads of our own day.

We preachers are the merchants of foolishness (1 Cor. 1:18–21). Our calling has been fictionalized as our shame. Preaching has been maligned in novels, plays, and the cinema until the culture seems to have abandoned all respect for us. Yet, for all our reputation, what other art could hold such glory? What other bridge could know such epoch-vaulting piers? Here in plain sermons, we humble preachers hold concourse with Hittites who traveled from Hermon to Hebron and never knew a Hyatt. Preaching alone calls out the great similarities of age-locked peoples. We are not so different after all. We, like them, are in need: We need to know God and how to relate to him. We are like those ancient God-needers in another way. We all have a fondness for stories. We are storytellers, story hearers, and, indeed, story writers. Their ancient precepts may divide us, but their stories make us one.

I recently met a Shiite Muslim woman who lives near our church. In meeting her, I became aware that our religious backgrounds were so different that we had very little about which we could talk. I perceive myself to be a fairly zealous Christian, and she was, without a doubt, a zealous Muslim. To be congenial, I had worked at pronouncing her name, Sherzhad. I could tell I was not doing a good job

144

of it. She helped me anglicize her name and then told me that it could also be pronounced Scheherazade.

After that her name came alive! Scheherazade is the name of a fabled harem princess whose sultan every morning executed his latest one-night stand. Not Scheherazade! At the end of her one-night stand, she told the sultan a fascinating tale. Like an old Baghdad rerun of "As the Muslim World Turns," however, she stopped her tantalizing episode with "to be continued." Even though the sultan wanted to get on with morning-after executions, he couldn't stand to kill her, not knowing how her story ended. His need to know prevailed over his need for sexual conquests. For once in history, story conquered eros, and Scheherazade lived to tell the story, or rather a thousand stories. Naturally the sheik kept her. He was mad about stories. So are we all. Our pulpit stories should be as captivating as Scheherazade's.

His Story

Our sermon illustrations are more than just idle tales. Our stories are oral events and presume a fixed point in time and space. The fairy tales of our childhood all include a "Once upon a time." They do so because the storyteller is trying to say it is important that all hearers fix the tales in some land and some time. Our pulpit illustrations need a definite framework to set our stories in firm significance.

In preaching, the best part of storytelling focuses on some portion of the Scripture story. Unlike sermon illustrations, Bible stories are history. They are not just any-old-Toynbee kind of factual history. They are special history. The Bible is the tale of God and people intertwined. It relates how they walked with God and were with God. This saving story begins, however, at a fixed time and place. The fixing point is Eden, somewhere near the Tigris, Euphrates, Nile, or Yalu rivers. Who can say? The time of the beginning is "Once upon a time," clearly labeled at the starting point: *B'reshith barah Elohim* . . . "In the beginning God . . ." *B'reshith barah Elohim*—the primeval once-upon-a-time words. The Gospel narratives also begin with a

145

Greek "once upon a time": "In the beginning was the Word, and the Word was with God . . . and we have seen his glory, the glory of the One and Only, who came from the Father, full of grace and truth" (John 1:1, 14).

Words are the basic units of stories, and the stories begin in Genesis and run through the Apocalypse. There is some question about whether our pulpit stories are primarily oral or visual events. Paul saw the gospel as a hearing event: "Faith cometh by hearing, and hearing by the word of God" (Rom. 10:17 KJV). When the sermon words combine, they form not only oral events but visual images in our minds. Real plots, real characters, and real images are the components of our saving story.

Christianity is regarded as a literary religion. J. B. Broadbent said in his introduction to *Paradise Lost*: "Christianity is the most literary religion in the world: it is crammed with characters and stories."[1] Even as the Bible is replete with stories, our sermons will best reflect the narrative style of Scripture when they also become narrative.

If Christianity is literary, can it be said to be wholly literary? The word *literature* presupposes imagination. We must remember that although the novel is a comparatively recent development, myths and fables were common in the Greco-Roman world. The classic myths were based upon the interrelationships of gods and people. Even these myths were not seen to be wholly contrivances but rather explanations for the coming and going of nations, customs, seasons, and circumstances. By stirring mythology into their national story, the Greeks and Romans kept their history from being mundane. Thus their stories acquired a literary timelessness, couched in intrigue.

In a similar way, the Bible is more than literature. The stories that it tells are not make-believe. They do, however, reflect the polished art of raconteurs who first told them orally. Only later did these stories acquire their written literary genius. Evangelicals adore Scripture but as a whole have not been very integrated in world literature. The Bible is true, and we like true stories. Unfortunately, our justified love of Scripture has often caused us to trivialize other story sources.

Many evangelicals see novels only as well-told lies, but let us remember that the art of storytelling belongs to storytellers. Pablo Picasso said: "We all know that Art is not truth. Art is a lie that makes us realize truth."[2] The Bible is literature, and while it is not a lie, it is a well-told story that makes us realize the kind of truth that matters most. The biblical story, however, also interacts strongly with our own.

Our Story

All of us from Adam on are fairly aware that the human race is writing a story. That is perhaps why we are so fond of the Bible. If God had merely written all of his Word to us as golden precept-oriented proverbs, would we have been so interested? No. God is the great Narrator. Consider the frequency of all the biblical "once-upon-a-times":

Once upon a time, there was Adam and Eve and a serpent with a glittering fruit in his fangs. They did not live so happily ever after.

Once upon a time there was Noah, to whom the Lord God gave a hammer, saw, and cubit stick and said, "Go thou and build the Queen Mary!"

Once upon a time there was Nimrod and Methuselah and Abraham of Ur.

Once upon a time there was the wily Delilah and the gullible Samson.

Once upon a time there was Rahab of Jericho and Jonah blubbering in a fish's maw.

Once upon a time there was Jesus and Herod and a wee little man and Lazarus, who couldn't stay dead for long in the presence of the living Christ!

147

Once upon a time there was Peter and Paul and Priscilla and Pontius Pilate and a preacher of parables of peasants and power and pestilence.

Why do the narratives of Scripture so enthrall us? I believe it's because the biblical stories are so germane to the life narratives we ourselves are writing. "Once upon a time . . . ourselves." It is the writing of this latter story that occupies our years. The unpublished saga of every life is of interest because we have no idea *how* it will end, or *when*. Life stories sometimes grind to a sudden stop. Some reach out for volumes.

Preachers and the foolishness of preaching interpret life stories. Here and there, against every unfinished autobiography, comes the preacher, the troubadour. This all-important jongleur, as Francis of Assisi put it, takes the stories of Scripture and feeds them homiletically into other life scripts.

What comes of this blend? How does mixing the tales of ancient patriarchs, sheiks, bedouins, teachers, and preachers come to bear on current life? Stories speak to stories, and their ancient spells instruct and change, break and transform. Like shamans, preachers cause the world to see the reality of another mysterious world. Thus, gloriously, we preachers become "seers" at the center of community. Preacher storytellers are glorious participants *in* and the explainers *of* the narrative of God's revelation. We are called to bring the Bible story to bear on the life stories of our flocks. We then apply. We use the sermons to say, "See, here is how your story is like that of Adam, or Ruth, or Job, or Jonah, or Jethro, or Jepthah, or Judas, or John, or Jacob, or Jesus. You don't like how your life story is going? Then repent, retreat, resign, rewrite, or rejoice! Nevertheless, our urgent stories demand response."

When the flock does hear and change, we say, "Come, give your testimony. Tell us your story. Sing us your story in a hymn":

> I was lost in sin
> But Jesus rescued me
> He's a wonderful Savior to me.

148

The power inherent in pulpit stories always tends to make our hearers want to put their encounter with gospel stories in their own metaphors. The specific gospel story we herald fits everybody differently; so we cry out to the butcher, the baker, and the candlestick maker: "Here's a gospel story that can fit your specific vocation and need. Put it in your own words, but believe it."

Metaphorize your story; you're a mariner:
My soul in sad exile was out on life's seas . . .
And I entered that haven of rest.

Metaphorize, you're a railroad engineer:
Life is like a mountain railway
With an engineer that's brave.

Metaphorize, you're a tenement dweller:
Have you talked to the man upstairs?

Metaphorize, you're a cowboy:
Headin' for the last roundup.

Metaphorize, you're a Second Infantry recruit:
You're marching to Zion.

Metaphorize, you're a vagabond:
Guide me, O thou great Jehovah.

Metaphorize, you're sheep bleating high on a mountain:
He leadeth me,
O blessed thought.

Simile, please, you're back in Genesis 28, trying to get into heaven the hard way:
We are climbing Jacob's ladder.

149

All of us? On one ladder? Don't get so literal!

Amy-Semple-McPhersonize:
He's Calvary's crimson rose.

Stamps-Baxterize:
There's a sweet and blessed book
Tho' it's worn and faded now
That recalls those happy days.

Pop-Gospelize:
Oh, it won't be old Buddha
That's sittin' on the throne.

Latinize:
Venite Adoremus.

Anglicanize:
In the cross of Christ I glory.

Africanize:
Kum ba Yah.

Airlinize:
I'll fly away, oh glory.

Broadwayize:
Jesus Christ, Superstar,
Who are you, what do you say you are?

Gospel cable-dish satellite-ize:
Something good is going to happen to you.

Leave a little witness on the interstate:
   Honk if you love Jesus.

Our testimony is our story, set within the confines of our own unique province. No sooner are we born again than we begin to tell our children stories, and our little ones sing in rapture those ever-singable stories:

"Away in a manger, no crib for a bed . . ."
"Peter, James, and John in a little sailboat . . ."
"The wise man built his house upon the rock . . ."
"Bring a torch Jeanette Isabella . . ."
"When I play my drum, rum-pa-pum-pum . . ."
"Zacchaeus was a wee little man . . ."
"Only a boy named David . . ."

Thus adult story lovers propagate their love of stories from generation to generation.

The Storytellers

The stern rebukes of totally precept-focused preachers warn us from the use of story: "Give us only precept sermons, lest people remember your stories and miss your precepts." For years I have been testing this hypothesis. In fact, I have often bragged that I could tell what seminary a preacher was from just by listening to him preach and noticing what he did with story. If his sermons were bristling with common life and filled with very relational stories, he was doubtless not from any seminary, but streetwise from observing life on the "front." His stories hold a simple charm, uncluttered by education. I do not understand his homiletics, but such uneducated preachers often know that life is as warm as a bedtime story. The rule of their preachment seems to be, "Go ye into all the world and illustrate."

151

Sermons without any stories translate as cold as the black tungsten filament of projector bulbs. Overhead projectors are often their ensigns. The Ten Commandments, once written in fire, are at last written only on acetate with grease pencil. Where precept preempts stories, note taking is vogue. Harold Freeman calls this sermon style the "oral-exegesis style." The totally oral-exegesis sermon is culpable on these counts: First, it is guilty of notebook academics. Such preachers are fascinated by who the Antichrist is or where the ten lost tribes might have gone once they left Assyria. They can get so excited over the letter of the text that they spend weeks on God, Magog, or the great whole of the Apocalypse. Harry Emerson Fosdick saw such preachers as exegetical technicians who "assume that everyone still comes to church just dying to know whatever happened to the Hittites."

A second fault of oral exegetes is that they have a notebook theology. I had a friend who audiovisualized everything. He was always preaching on such subjects as: "The Lord, our great High Priest before the throne" on the same Sunday I was trying to deny that Big Bird was a humanist. This precept preacher was always prone to spend weeks explaining the dimensions of the New Jerusalem. In his way of seeing things, these details were important.

The third and worst fault of oral exegetes is their notebook arrogance. A little learning is a dangerous thing. Preachers can exalt academic truth to such a degree that they soon find themselves exalted as authorities on Scripture. Stories are too relational to promote such academic demagoguery. When the academic spirit takes charge, we are easily led toward such a thorough treatment of Scripture that we belabor the exegesis. One such preacher I read about spent a marathon forty-three weeks in Philippians. One of his less enchanted members, whose notebooks looked thin and atheistic, said, "The series is done, and while I still love my pastor, I hate the Book of Philippians."

Preaching precepts now dominate the worship style of many congregations. There where bulbs are cooled by the slight bump of tiny fans, Hebrew word roots come and go, along with their Aramaic and Greek counterparts. Outlines with subpoints rising like the horns of the beast come and go. Ballpoint pens glide over columnar pads, leaving in their wake definitions of dispensation and triangular graphics explaining the Trinity. In overhead projector-ese, it is the *rhema* word that steals the attention of the *logos* word to the point that academics replace adoration. Precept preaching then gets so one-dimensional that it leaves no place for preaching as craft.

Further, precept preaching promotes a love for the Word as word and often fails to teach that the Word exists to confront and change. It is reminiscent of rabbis whose ritual exalts the Torah, kissing it and returning it to the tabernacle where it will live with a muted respect that never makes any demands. This is particularly true in the teaching church that has no altar inviting decisions based upon the demand of the Scripture text.

Does story need to obliterate precept-oriented note giver? No. I am convinced story would punctuate any sermon with interest. It would soften the academic harshness of sermonic dictum. Remember, the Word is more than word; the Word has been made flesh! How did the Word-made-flesh preach? He had no overhead projector. Would he have used one if he had come after Edison? I think not. Jesus' sermons do not labor over word roots. Jesus did not exegete for fifty-five minutes nor dissect any Old Testament word. The Sermon on the Mount is his only entire sermon reproduced in the Bible, and it can be preached in eighteen minutes. In an economy of 2,320 words, Jesus spends 348 on such images as wolves, sheep, light, rock, sand, and storms.

We rarely take notes during stories. Notes are the inky tracks of precept preaching. Pencils and pads have a way of keeping hands so busy that minds do not notice they are sleepy. In churches where note taking is essential to self-esteem, the entire congregation may need to ask, "Without my pencil and pad, could I stand to listen one hour to him?"

I believe there often operates a kind of martyr complex in some oral-exegete churches. Their consensus is that Scripture sermons should be austere and no fun. Indeed, some seem to feel that listening to a sermon is a cross to be carried. To actually enjoy a sermon is evidence of its shallowness. "So," they seem to cry, "make us learn Greek roots and complex schematics lest we enjoy our Christianity and demonstrate our utter superficiality." Maybe a story would help.

I have yet to be convinced that story obliterates precept. In the Scriptures, story and precept come bound together. Take the Decalogue, ten marvelous precepts, but they come packaged in narration—splitting seas, bloody Passovers, Miriam's tambourine celebrations, Aaron's calf, and manna showers. Which is most important, story or precept? Well, they are inseparable. Likewise, the New Testament precepts come packaged in the many parables and narratives of Christ. So precepts are made to live often by the direct bearing of a story. Jesus, for instance, gives us some fascinating illustrations of light: "Don't put a candlestick under a bushel basket, and keep your cities on hilltops." The double whammy of this double metaphor is a precept: "Let your light shine!"

Biblical preaching in the Old Testament exults in narrative. Consider Elijah. If the story is told well, the precept becomes unnecessary. Saccharine stories usually lose their dramatic force. I once likened Jezebel, walking the lonely balustrades of Samaria with blood on her hands, to Lady Macbeth crying, "Out, damned spot." The president of the Woman's Missionary Union noticed the word. After the sermon she advised, "Whatever Lady Macbeth said, you should have told us she said, "'Oh, fiddlesticks.'" I disagree, Lady M. and Jezebel must both be allowed the force of their real-life drama.

Nathan stomps into the hypocritical monarch and says, "Let me tell you a story." David listens and grows indignant at his own sin when he sees it in the life of another. What would have happened if Nathan had never said, "Thou art the man"? My suspicion is that somewhere in time, when the palace was silent at midnight and Bathsheba had a headache or his mother-in-law was there for the second weekend in a row, the prophet's story would have haunted him. Lady Bathsheba would have wrung her hands like Lady Macbeth and cried over Uriah's blood, "Out, damned Hittite stains! Not all of Lake Gennesaret will wash clean these small hands!" Nathan's story was a scalding rebuke sent to cleanse a king's conscience. Great stories come to bear on lives sometimes in precept, sometimes in tears, but always in strong confrontation.

The story is glory! Are all raconteurs? To some degree, I think so! It is an art to tell a story well, yet it is an art never perfected. All who are called to preach are called to tell a story better. If you think you can't tell a story better, venture cautiously forward with tentative beginnings. You must first accept the importance of the story. Take any sermonic precept you wish. Repeat it a few times, and a certain drowsiness will begin to camp in your listeners' eyes. Ten more precepts without a story and the brightest eye begins to glaze, till finally the lids wax shut, jaws slacken, and minds separate themselves from the sermon altogether. Finally, even precepts die. The only precept that may call back a sleepy mind is the word "Fire!" shouted with sufficient force; it remains one of the few precepts that can interrupt a real storyteller.

Conclusion

Our stories must not only interest, they must motivate us to produce. There are some important questions to be asked of story.

Do Stories Produce Change?

Purely precept preachers criticize that stories interest but do not change lives. As I conclude, I argue that stories are the real life changers, for they *do* produce. Their first and most significant product is conversion. They also confront and change lives. They motivate to holiness, to prayer, and to a loving and continuing affair with Scripture.

Are Stories a Real Product?

Stories in sermons call attention to the creative. I once heard an oral exegete use the Greek word *poiema* from Ephesians 2:10 to say that new Christians are God's creation, his poems, something constructed, his workmanship. So our sermons are our art, our product, our creation. Sermons are product, but stories and storytelling must not be seen as mere product—that is, something to reward us at the back door with a compliment. Stories are the tools used to sculpt better lives.

Is Storytelling a Special Talent?

I think not. Anyone can learn to tell stories to some degree. Stories are already there. The artistry comes in seeing and feeling all that exists around us. Artists cannot walk through their world without feeling it rub against them. In that rubbing, artistry is born. We who preach must also learn to see the common things that others pass by. This "bypass" is usable in homiletics.

Pulitzer Prize winner Annie Dillard watched a mockingbird leap from the roof gutter of a four-story building.

> The mockingbird took a single step into the air and dropped. His wings were still folded against his sides as though he were singing from a limb and not falling, accelerating thirty-two feet per second through empty air. Just a breath before he would have been dashed to the ground, he unfurled his wings with exact, deliberate care, revealing the broad bars of white, spread his elegant, white-banded tail, and so floated onto the grass. I had just rounded a corner when his insouciant step caught my eye; there was no one else in sight. The fact of this free fall was like the old philosophical conundrum about the tree that falls in the forest. The answer must be, I think, that beauty and grace are performed whether or not we will or sense them. The least we can do is try to be there.[3]

Such stories as this are common in the life of the man or woman tuned to little things. Little things were the fabric of Jesus' stories. Flowers, sandy foundations, rent collectors, and muggers in and around Jericho were what he talked about. Did they hear him? Of course! The Scriptures say that the common people heard him with delight (Mark 12:37).

Jesus was heard because, like Annie Dillard, when he saw a sparrow fall to the ground, something within his heart snapped. Was he alone at prayer the day it happened? Did our Lord, with Audubon awareness, watch an old sparrow wing-split the Galilean air for the last illustration? He knew the feathers were needed by the earth to make humus. Life had to give itself, sparrow-fashion, so that the ground into which it fell would celebrate newness. Still, the Son of God knew his Father was a sparrow lover. Jesus had come to show others what it is like to die. Being Son of God, he watched the sparrow, brittle of bone and beak, crash into the coarse earth. The feathers heaved as though they might rise once more. Finally they shuddered, relaxed, and lay, down-soft in the morning. Jesus perhaps suffered one of the unrecorded tears in Scripture: "Are not two sparrows sold for a penny? Yet not one of them will fall to the ground apart from the will of your Father" (Matt. 10:29).

We are gathering our art by being in the world and gratefully seeing all that is around us. Perceiving life is preparing to preach. When sermons come from men and women with no perception, the eye of the hearer is blinded, the ear is filled with the wax of oratory that never touched the world. T. S. Eliot judged such waxy oratory: "All our knowledge is only bringing us closer to our ignorance; . . . What is the life we have lost in living?"4 The preacher must answer that question.

We who preach are the divine raconteurs, telling the "old, old story" by telling loads of new, new stories. These stories will get at truth, motivate the productive life, and drive out the demons of boredom. Thus the world will learn of God and cheer that we have held its attention while it learned.

10

The Story as Ultimate Truth

But note how in a story located in space and time the polarities of abstract/concrete and general/specific are overcome. The story moves through inner and outer action, development of character, and progression plot—and by so doing, the extremes of abstract and concrete are merged into event. . . . And the form story takes transcends such polarities with power because that's the way we actually live our own lives.

Eugene L. Lowry

Fairy stories are "spiritual explorations" and hence "the most life-like" since they reveal "human life as seen, or felt, or divined from the inside."

Bruno Bettelheim

Little Red Riding Hood was my first love. I felt that if I could have married Little Red Riding Hood, I should have known perfect bliss.

Charles Dickens

We established in chapter 9 that it is unwise to be either a precept *or* a storytelling preacher. Rather, those two sermon elements go together. Storytelling preaching is from the right brain. It is kept in line by the left brain. You cannot have preaching without both sides cooperating.

I used to picture in my mind that when graduates left seminary to take their place in the world, some would leave with a tambourine and a portfolio of choruses. Others would leave with a notebook and an interlinear Bible. Some would publish joy, others information. Some would tell stories, others would preach fearsome precepts. If the world were so easily divisible into story churches and precept churches, I think both of them, well done, would be equally popular to two very different groups for two very different reasons. As a story preacher, I freely admit that precept churches can grow very well. Nearly every city has at least one great precept church. They fulfill a great need; they are churches that teach the Bible, and their singular dedication to the task is worthy.

These large precept churches exist because some people, wearied by rambling, pointless sermons, have come to feel that truth—even overhead-projector truth—is better than no truth at all. All preachers are scattered equally along the precept-to-story gradient. There are likely as many precept-oriented preachers as storytellers. We almost can't help our natural inclinations. Our Myers-Briggs inventory, I suspect, will tell us loads about our personality functions. It will show us not only what kind of preacher we are, but what kind of preaching we enjoy.

People come to our churches looking for a reason to go on in life, a *raison d'être*. Only if our stories are "ultimate" can we speak to these extreme issues. Consider the great lines in ultimate story moments when narrative speaks to narrative.

> Dickens's Sidney Carton in *A Tale of Two Cities*, for instance, touches me when he stands at the guillotine to say, "It is a far, far better thing I do than I have ever done before. It is a far, far better rest to which I go."
>
> Shakespeare's Cardinal Wolsey also touches me in *Henry VIII* when he says, "If I had served my God half as well as I had served my

160

king, he would not in my time have left me naked to mine enemies."

Don Quixote touches me when he cries, "I've never had the courage to believe in nothing."

Lavinia, too, touches me when she lifts her baby to the cross of the dying Spartacus and cries, "Your son is free born!"

Yuri, the poet, driven by love, touches all of us when he scratches the name "Lara" in the icy halls at Varykino.

Spock in *The Wrath of Khan* touches me when he says through the steaming glass, "Admiral, the needs of the many outweigh the needs of the few." I gasped at the sacrifice of the noble Vulcan dying that others might live!

Ultimate stories tell life truths, truths that are so universal that they can speak to the smaller, particular truths of our hearts. Our members enter our churches with broken hearts; their life stories aren't working out. These attend us, filtering our sermons through their own crying needs. Dare we try to cure such pain with stories? For the person having a baby out of wedlock, the child abuser, or the cancer victim, our sermons must tell deeply serious stories that relate, encircle, and save.

Stories can relate many levels of truth, but pulpit stories must tell the truths that matter most. John Steinbeck said that there are two major literary symbols of the West: Jesus and Arthur of England.[1] I have asked myself why these two symbols are primary. I think it is because of the ultimacy of both stories. Jesus represents the story with a saved-ideal ending, and Arthur represents the story with the lost-ideal ending.

Tolkien, in his essay "On Faerie," said that there were only two possible story endings, one of which was *catastrophe* and the other *eucatastrophe*. The unhappy ending, catastrophe, is very iconoclast, smashing human hope and leaving readers with a kind of unsettled longing for resolution. Witness Arthur. The happy ending, eucatastrophe, rights all wrongs and calls every tale to an end that is content. Witness Jesus.

The happy ending (eucatastrophe), I believe, was born in the *evangelium*, the gospel story where the victimized, executed Jesus comes alive again in power. The resurrection puts Humpty Dumpty back together again. What would have been the greatest of all human tragedies becomes the happiest of all possible endings. We can all live happily ever after because of the resurrection ideal.

Teleios is the Greek word for completion. Completion is the finest answer we may give to our search for meaning. There is something in us that resents unfinished novels. We all want settled conclusions to critical issues. We want stories, and certainly sermons, to end with recognizable conclusions of hope.

There is some evidence that Paul, while he is the progenitor of much of Western Christendom, did not know how to conclude a sermon. "Woe to me if I do not preach the gospel," cried the apostle (1 Cor. 9:16). It is a pity the critical Corinthians didn't feel that way. They were honest sermon critics: "His letters are weighty and forceful, but in person he is unimpressive and his speaking amounts to nothing" (2 Cor. 10:10). The Corinthians prove that the thing we tend to remember most about preachers is how long their sermons are. John Hersey, in "God's Typhoon," commented on Dr. Wyman's sermons. His theology was harsh, his sermons long and brutal: "His interminable sermons at the Union Church came at us in an insistent singsong, half whine, half roar, and my restlessness in the pews on those Sabbath mornings was edged with dread."[2]

Waiting for the end of sermons in the Pentecostal church where I was converted was pure hell. Sister Rose, our pastor, would stand enraptured, hands uplifted, face upturned, eyes closed in ecstasy. I couldn't tell what she was seeing, but I envisioned her focusing on a great gold wristwatch on the arm of Methuselah, who had already done his time in church. She said eternity would be wonderful—running on, as it did, forever—but I wasn't sure. Way back then, I made up my mind that while the glory of eternity was that it never ended, the glory of preaching was that it did, and I only liked those preachers whose sermons let me watch as they neared the finish line. While I could never talk in tongues, the final, one o'clock "amen" always brought me closest to ecstatic utterance.

Why did I stay to the end? For the same reason my parishioners now stay; I was hungry for truth. The entire Bible is future oriented, and the sum total of all the stories in the Bible is that their fullest interpretation can only come in the future. The Scripture *teleios* is that final finishing which is yet to come. The future shall see all injustice terminated and every tear dried. The Bible, from first to last, underscores this thesis: *The future shall not be lost as a place of hope.*

Tom Stoppard's *Rosencrantz and Guildenstern Are Dead* may have reached popularity because it focuses entirely on two tiny roles from Shakespeare's *Hamlet*. To read *Hamlet*, one can only ask, "Who are these seldom-appearing nobodies, Rosencrantz and Guildenstern?" In their own play, which briefly intersects *Hamlet*, one sees these two hapless souls lost in a search for enduring truth. Nobody is so minor in life that his personal story is minor to himself. Rosencrantz and Guildenstern are not minor roles to Rosencrantz and Guildenstern.

In a way, Rosencrantz and Guildenstern are coping with "worm theology." The legacy of John Calvin may be to teach that humankind are but worms before a holy God, but we want to see more in ourselves than that. So Stoppard stops the action, and for a couple of hours Rosencrantz and Guildenstern get a chance to evaluate their wormhood and take the issue, "To be or not to be," upon themselves. It is only fair. After all, Hamlet got his chance. They are major actors striving with their own right to hope, to dream, to stand at last on the top of their circumstances.

Consider these facets of final truth:

Ultimate truth is the only one that matters.
Ultimate truth is nonreducible.
Ultimate truth is common sense.
Story becomes the ultimate metaphor of our life.

These facets of hope are best proclaimed when story preaching and powerful precepts join ranks.

Ultimate Truth Is the Only One That Matters

Since great, irreducible truths are the truths that matter, no story should be allowed to spoil the gospel story. We storytellers are the gleaners—watching movies, reading plays, novels, and so forth. We're trying to glean secondary narratives that will help tell the primary epic. Not all stories are friendly to this telling. In my inordinate hunger to know everything about every novel or play, I have had to watch what I ingest. It does little good to corrupt the heart in order to build an imaginative mind. The Spirit cannot live in a corrupt heart. If the heart is X-rated, the richest imagination cannot serve Christ, and thus the sermon's usefulness will be captive to the world. None can tell another how far to push reading habits. Our hearts alone can tell, and the Spirit must be our guide.

The Dixie pulpit has given us the legacy of the sermon that sounds serious. Usually it's not the sermon's theme that is serious; it is only its sound. One can see the screwed-up faces, the pumping gestures, and the steel cheeks of video cyborgs and tell the sound is serious. Yet sound never answers need. Meaning comes through inner dialogue, not by outer thunder.

One can see why existentialism became a dominant philosophy in our century. Riddled by two world wars, we ever live with the threat of another. Our generation is obsessed with the need to identify the riddles of life and death, continuance and extinction. The existentialist novels and plays of Jean Paul Sartre, Albert Camus, Samuel Beckett, and Peter Shaffer evidence the futility of this search. Therefore, preaching blesses when it guarantees that the future *will* be there as a place of hope.

Where there's life, there's hope. Nonsense! Even our old clichés cannot be trusted. Where there's life, there is often despair. Where there's life, there's suicide, death wish, manic depression, tears, bereavement, unwanted pregnancy, scandal, embezzlement, and AIDS. We must erect the brazen serpent at each service and say, "Look and live." It's the best way our brief homilies can confront human meaninglessness.

One cliché really speaks to the importance of the story in sermon: "I'm having a better time in life since I've given up all hope." This bumper-sticker proverb called to my mind again what a heavy burden there is in hoping. Hoping is the oft-disappointing and disillusioning work of human existence. Hoping is the heart of Gepetto in the children's fable. To have his little Pinocchio, his wondrous "Wooden eyes," is the dream of the lonely old puppet maker. The adolescent Pinocchio, however, is a hardwood heartbreaker. He shoots up, goes to adult theaters, and fills his oaken heart with wooden concern. He is not a genuine son, but a replica, whose face is cheap veneer and whose nose grows long with lust for lying image. At last, Gepetto cries, and so do many parents as child crime by child crime, their dreams die. A neighbor's daughter is in prison for life. She never speaks of her without tears, like lava through stone, cutting across her face. Perhaps to keep her hopes from dying, God gave the world the sermon. Come, Gepetto, listen and believe, God also had a Son and that's a wondrous story of hope.

Being always loses out to *time*, unless the Lord of time is made the Lord of being. Everyone is reckoning with time and struggling against the clock. They cry their elemental hungers in church, "I don't want to die, but I've swallowed the hemlock. Please help me!" To this cry we reply, "Come to the sermon. We study hope here every Sunday at eleven. You will both hear and remember this hope. We case it in narratives powerful enough to change your life."

Ultimate Truth Is Nonreducible

Einstein's formula, $E = mc^2$, is significant because it relates energy and matter, and it does so in a final, nonreducible formula. Theology also deals with nonreducible formulas. At its heart, theology is not complex. It yearns to take the complexity of the human milieu and simplify it, but to say it is simple is not to write if off as insignificant.

A widely quoted story tells of an Ivy League school where a theologian and an astronomer were belittling each other's sciences: "'Now let's face it,' said the astronomy professor, 'in religion, what it all boils

165

down to very simply is that you should love your neighbor as your-self. It's the Golden Rule, right?' 'Yes, I suppose that's true,' answered the divinity school dean. 'Just as in astronomy it all boils down to one thing—"twinkle, twinkle, little star."'"[3]

Theology, like astronomy, can be oversimplified. Still, there is some-thing tremendous in any truth that makes it friends with all truth. Socrates said, "Aristotle is my friend. Plato is my friend, but my great-est friend is truth."

Ultimate Truth Is Common Sense

Most stories that have affected Western culture have a compelling common sense about them. Back to $E = mc^2$ a moment. This sim-ple formula has occupied the greatest physicists and mathematicians for years. Its simplicity was first revealed in a practical circumstance. Albert Einstein was waiting for a train, and as he waited he looked at a clock, reminding him of how long it would be till the train came. What would happen, he wondered, if the train could travel at the same speed as the light which was bringing the image of the clock dial to the retina of his eye? How would the train be altered? In such a simple nest, relativity hatched. I have never forgotten the precept $E = mc^2$ because I cannot get this story out of my mind.

Simplicity is where every story shines. We have long bragged that the gospel is a simple story. Jesus said it was hidden from the wise and revealed to little children (Matt. 11:25). At conversion, the power of the gospel story collides with our individual life story. The emo-tional smoke lifts, and we are saved. This salvation is the sunny coun-try of common sense. The saving story is fraught with mystery. It con-tains the great unanswerables of faith: God invading the womb of a virgin and being born a man. This God-man, in a trio of decades, would die on a cross and then, being dead for a trio of days, would rise again and go to the right hand of the Father on high. All of our pulpit stories rise from a heart of paradox. They are at once common sense and utter mystery. Between their mystery and their common sense, our stories express the entirety of all meaning.

I once led to Christ a logical young man who loved the "sunny country of common sense" but agonized over the mysteries of faith. He kept shoving common sense at me while I kept trying to nourish him with mystery. One day he said to me, "Pastor, you know this new, eternal life I have?"

"Yes," I replied.

"Well," he continued, "I've been thinking. What are we going to do all day long for eternity?"

I immediately remembered Huck Finn and Miss Watson. It was a fair question. Given the end of the Sunday school board, seminary commissions, and the inerrancy debate, what *will* we do all day?

"Well," I said, "we will praise the Lord for eternity." It sounded a little intimidating, even to me.

"For eternity? . . . Forever and ever? . . . For ten million years, we are just going to stand around and praise the Lord?"

"Well, yes," I said, although heaven was beginning to sound like cable television.

"For millions and millions of years?" he went on. "Couldn't we just stop and mess around once in a while?"

"Maybe." I quickly walked away, feeling the undeniable tension between doctrine and mystery.

Ultimate stories have ultimate effects on our lives. Shakespeare's Hamlet uses a device of truth, *The Murder of Gonzago*. It is a play that a troop of actors in *Hamlet* perform within the main drama, a play within a play. It is really a marvelous piece of gestalt. Hamlet substituted a half-dozen of his own lines to show a murder that parallels his uncle's murder of his father. As the play continues, his uncle's reaction clearly shows that he is guilty of the crimes Hamlet suspects. Claudius does what we all do in the presence of any story. We compare our life story with the one we are reading or seeing. It is not Claudius alone who is affected by the story. Hamlet seizes his mother, thrusts her into a chair and says,

> Come, come, and sit you down, you shall not budge!
> You go not till I shall set you up a glass
> Where you may see the inmost part of you.[4]

167

Stories always fall into two categories: *amusement* (those stories that keep our minds occupied while we sit idle) and *gestalt models* (those stories that impact our selves at deeper psychological levels, thus they become life changing). The gestalt story lays down one demand: "Do not merely listen to me, use me as a surgeon would use a scalpel. I am story, sent to cut, excise, and heal. I am both reasonable and transforming, sent to lead you to the sunny country of common sense."

Stories Become the Ultimate Metaphor of Life

Lines, plots, images, and characters, by their very mention, furnish us much of the script for living. For instance, we so often say:

"My hometown was 'Peyton Place,' pure 'Harper Valley PTA.'"
"His life is 'Rags to Riches,' 'Prince and the Pauper' stuff."
"He has an 'Oedipus' complex," or, "She has a 'Cinderella' complex."
"That is an ant-and-grasshopper philosophy."
"He's a 'rebel without a cause.'"
"The whole situation is a 'comedy of errors.'"
"That was a pyrrhic victory."
"Don't be so Trafalgar."
"He met his Waterloo that time."
"Well, if it isn't the Lone Ranger."
"Life is certainly Camelot when it's not the pit and the pendulum."

Story plots define life situations, and characters define our relationships. We all know Hueys, Deweys, Louies, Ebenezer Scrooges, Pollyannas, and Little Lord Fauntleroys. We all know Nicholas Nicklebys in quest of themselves, Captain Marvels, and Garfields. Who hasn't faced down some power-hungry Uriah Heep or chauvinistic Archie Bunker? It is a great compliment to be called a Mother Teresa, but not a Sadie Thompson. Stories become the way we describe ourselves in various situations. They are the guiding metaphors of our lives.

As stories are life metaphors, so are they death metaphors. Indeed, stories are the fundamental metaphors of dying. It has been well said that no religion is worth a copper that doesn't teach us how to die. Noble dying is the theme of the best life stories. Can we not admire how Prince Andrew died in *War and Peace,* or even Anna Karenina's suicide in Tolstoy's other great novel? Who cannot grieve the plaintive dying of Little Nell in *The Old Curiosity Shop?* I wept at the broad hilt of Excalibur being received by the Lady of the Lake. Was not part of you lost when Matthew clutched his chest in *Anne of Green Gables?* Powerful images monitor our dying—President Kennedy's riderless steed behind the coffin and the caisson in the long, proud, empty walk to Arlington; Horatio weeping his "Good night, sweet prince, and flights of angels sing thee to thy rest." More than once, Verona's quarrel has left me weeping over senseless riots. I hear the deep voice of the narrator crying over dead lovers:

> A glooming peace this morrow with it brings
> That sure for sorrow will not show his head
> For never was tale more filled with woe
> Than this of Juliet and her Romeo.[5]

Death has a million metaphors and stories—Lear holding the dead Cordelia, Othello grieving his lost Desdemona, Marcellus at the stake.

Malcolm Muggeridge speaks of the coming victory of his own death as "seeing beyond the iron gates."[6] This wonderful final vision can exist when we consider the story as final truth *(teleios).* We shall, or rather Christ shall, break the iron gates that seal us from the sunny country of common sense.

Conclusion

Preachers we are. We are the story makers, the makers of hope, the makers of irreducible meaning. Nowhere are stories more basic in meaning than in the funeral sermon. The funeral sermon is the best place to test our theories. Here the story is glory. Withhold this ultimate story and we cannot teach the glory of ultimate life that triumphs over mere decades of temporal life.

Walt Whitman constantly sang of meaning. His life was marked with pain, paralysis, and heavy silence:

> I sit and look out upon all the sorrows of the
>   world, and upon all oppression and shame,
> I hear secret convulsive sobs from young men at
>   anguish with themselves, remorseful after deeds
>   done,
> I see in low life the mother misused by her
>   children, dying, neglected, gaunt, desperate,
> I see the wife misused by her husband, I see the
>   treacherous seducer of young women,
> I mark the ranklings of jealousy and unrequited
>   love attempted to be hid, I see these sights
>   on the earth,
> I see the working of battle, pestilence, tyranny,
>   I see martyrs and prisoners, . . .
> All these—all the meanness and agony without end
>   I sitting look out upon,
> See, hear, and am silent.[7]

Before ultimate truth we are silent.

11

The Story as Relational Truth

Preaching the biblical word today cannot take on a peopleless monotone when such a story of people's stories is its authority.

F. Dean Lueking

In a less grandiose vein, students today have nothing like the Dickens who gave so many of us the unforgettable Pecksniffs, Micawbers, Pips, with which we sharpened our vision, allowing us some subtlety in our distinction of human types. It is a complex set of experiences that enables one to say so simply, "He is a Scrooge." Without literature, no such observations are possible and the fine art of comparison is lost.

Allan Bloom

Our personhood, grounded in the authority of the Word we proclaim, is always relational.

F. Dean Lueking

Precept and story must serve together, getting precepts from lobe to lobe—from the lobe of the speaker to the lobe of the listener. Stories lubricate this transfer. Precepts build doctrinal coherence, but nothing has the strong relational power of stories. If one is ever prone to doubt the relational power of stories, consider how the release of a film generates a nation full of enthusiastic conversationalists overnight.

Christians for so many centuries now have found unity in the Apostles' Creed, a story confession. Believing in the Father and in Jesus Christ, his Son (who was born of a virgin, who died under Pontius Pilate, who rose again from the dead and is seated at the right hand of the Father) is a story confession that has united Christians across the centuries. Conversion and martyrdom always focus around the importance of the central story of a faith. Conversion is an attempt to get people to change stories. Martyrdom often comes as a result of not being willing to give up that story.

Precepts, then, are the skeletal systems upon which we hang our stories of faith. Back when I was taking college anatomy, we had a skeleton, dubbed Caroline, in our classroom. Caroline had a hinged jaw. We could pull down her jaw and stick a lollipop in it. We often taped a rose to her skull to give her a bony femininity. One of my fellow students was an attractive woman named Bonnie. Bonnie and Caroline had a lot of things in common. I knew that they were structurally alike, but I dated Bonnie. Perhaps this example says enough about how precept and story differ, and why precept alone lacks intrigue.

A decade ago I removed the pulpit from the chancel of our church. Two deacons lugged it back in, saying that the pulpit had come from the Bonham estate and shouldn't be removed. So we compromised and put it in the basement. It was a fearsome step for me, preaching without a pulpit. Some in our church said that pulpits symbolized authority. "So does the Berlin Wall," I replied. "I do this to take a step in favor of relationships, not authority." So the wall was down, and there we stood, face to face, preacher and people. Perhaps authority did suffer a bit. John Stott once said that pulpits were places where preachers stood tall and preached eight feet above contradiction. Without the sacred wall, some authority ebbed, but my relationship with the congregation also grew.

172

Carl Sandburg was once asked what was the ugliest word in the English language. Sandburg, in a way only he could do it, repeated the question: "The ugliest word? The ugliest word?" He said it a third time, "The very ugliest word?" When he had everybody's attention, he quietly dropped the egg into the nest and said, "Exclusive."[1]

The most beautiful word, I think, must be the word *friend,* for *friend* is inclusive. Being relational in the pulpit is an imperative the contemporary preacher dare not ignore. When every show is a talk show and every discussion is a panel discussion, the age declares that it is sociologically hungry. *Relationship* has become an all-important word. In his book *A Different Drum,* M. Scott Peck examines the idea of community as the crying need of the twentieth century.[2] The need to learn has been superseded in every organization by our need to fit in. Preaching, therefore, must be dialogue. The sermon as monologue is dead.

Stories and Individual or Group Identity

Eugene Peterson says that we keep telling stories "to locate ourselves in the human condition."[3] Story is the mortar of relationships. Story binds the soul of families or nations. As a child, I liked the stories of my Grandma Kent, whose first name was Sadie and whose middle name was Nebraska. "Why Nebraska?" I once asked her.

"Because I was born in a covered wagon in Nebraska in 1882," Grandma replied. "We were on the way to settle somewhere out West when my father turned south to Oklahoma." I loved the simple story. In 1940, 1882 seemed a long time ago. Whenever Grandma would come to northern Oklahoma, I wanted to hear that story again. My grandmother would once more tell me how she happened to become Sadie Nebraska Kent. Grandma died in 1951, and my mother and I would often talk about our prairie heritage. Mother, who had been born in Oklahoma territory herself, never tired of telling our Indian territory heritage. In time, I returned to Nebraska to be a pastor. My own children were born in the state that was part of Grandmother's name. From time to time, I told my children of their great-grand-mother, Sadie Nebraska, and, of course, they loved the story.

Why tell this story at all? Stories locate us in the human condition, and stories bind families to each other and the earth. Sadie Nebraska Kent helped me find my place in time. The stories of primitive nations are usually the sagas of clans, for most nations are but single families grown large. At the beginning of the tale of Rome is the story of the quarreling twins Romulus and Remus. At the beginning of the tale of the Anasazi Indian culture of the American Southwest is the emergence of life from the spirit-womb of Sipapu. At the beginning of the Hebrew nation is the call of one who may have been a moon worshiper, Abram of Ur, with Sarai his wife. Sometimes these stories by which a people remember their origin are mythical, sometimes true. Whether they are true or myth, story becomes the mortar of cultural relationships.

It is the accretions, however, that so intrigue us. Accretions interweave legend and history so that we cannot tell them apart. Did Davy Crockett really kill a bear when he was only three? Although I have seen vicious, unruly children in church nurseries, I doubt it. Did Beowulf really dispatch Grendel's mother? Is half of what they say about Pendragon and Igraine of Tintagel true? Did Arthur use the round table to invent parliament or backgammon? Such genesis epics, like rolling snowballs, gain bulk as they are told and retold; the kernel of the story encrusts itself with myth and romance. Thus cultural-identity stories become highly specialized and ethnic. Thus different cultures celebrate their origins as they celebrate their uniqueness, marking and defining who they are as a people.

This is certainly as true of Christianity as it would be for other religions. We have our story: Once upon a time Jesus, once upon a time a cross, a tomb. Once upon a time Easter. Once upon a time the greatest story ever told. We feel intensely protective of our story, as do other cultures. We feel others cannot be saved unless they believe our story is true, as do other religions.

Ayn Rand once said that art is man defining himself. It is true that the stories we tell from the pulpit define ourselves. Mention

Huck Finn, and we think of Mark Twain. Mention Billy Budd, and we think of Herman Melville. Each of these stories is the definition of its tellers. The stories that define nations are strong and well defended. Arthur defines primitive England. Miles Standish and Paul Revere are our American stories. Jubilation T. Cornpone is the rallying saga of Dogpatch patriotism. I'm not sure Eva Peron is the defining story of Argentina for Argentines, but every time I hear "Don't Cry for Me, Argentina," I want to cry for Argentina, and since I hardly ever want to cry for Bolivia or Paraguay, I suspect the art of Andrew Lloyd Webber's story defines the nation for me.

For all of us, story becomes the definition—sometimes the hard definition—of our lives. Stories draw firm lines of prejudice and hate. Men and women draw symbols of their stories—Christian crosses, Davidic stars, Muslim moons, Shinto suns—and march, singing battle anthems as their imperial story cries, "Become a convert to our faith, tear down your altars and shrines, replace them with ours! Change stories!"

It is often story loyalty that drives cultures apart, but the glory of living in a crowded world may at last teach us. Sheer numbers and international economics are producing the first tentative tolerance of each other's stories, and, at last, we recognize that to live together we must make allowances for different stories.

"East is East and West is West," wrote Rudyard Kipling, "and never the twain shall meet." Not so! They meet regularly in our shrinking world. Now that they are meeting, can our stories serve to make their meeting amenable? Any number of stories have risen to make the meeting easier. There will be later stories about East meeting West in a spirit of reconciliation and understanding. In making the story more global, two things will still be true: Preachers in our world system must remain the primary storytellers, and, as Philips Brooks says, truth will still have to come through the medium of personhood. So much depends upon the preacher as storyteller. To tell the old, old story to the brave new world, we will have to sharpen our skills and become the best of raconteurs.

Small Individual Stories and Wide Relationship

The whole world loves a story . . . and a storyteller. Some of my favorite memories of the late Grady Nutt, the Southern humorist, I earned by staring into his toothy grin and listening to him spin yarns. Deep in his Dixie baroque style there was ever truth. Grady wisely claimed that "to the storyteller belongs his or her art." I agree. A preacher's story should never lie, unless in the very telling of the lie there is such excess of language or hyperbole that it says clearly, "This is a lie, and while I tell it as though it were true, let's celebrate its fiction together." One feels, for instance, such hyperbole in the stories of Erma Bombeck. We know when she is lying, and she knows we know, but isn't it fun to enjoy the exaggeration together?

There is no need to ask Garrison Keillor if there really is a Chatter-Box Cafe; we know there is, and yet there isn't. There really isn't one in Lake Wobegon. In fact, there isn't a Lake Wobegon, Minnesota. Yet there was a similar cafe in Hunter, Oklahoma, where I had my first church. There is also a Val Tollofson, Keillor's Lutheran deacon, who couldn't see spending a nickel of the church's money on ideas that weren't his. I have met Val a half dozen times with as many names in many church business meetings.

Stories are symbols of things on which we are all agreed. What about this symbol: "Yes, Virginia, there really is a Santa Claus"? I suspect that there is. Does he fly? Mmm, okay. Have elves? Mmm, alright. In spite of the cancer-warning label on tobacco, Santa smokes, and he clearly overeats, risking a double bypass to remain a chubby cultural symbol. While many Southern fundamentalists point out that Santa is a humanist who is big on welfare and the United Fund, those who openly doubt Santa find themselves off a great many Christmas lists.

Symbols, fantasy or legend, mold us culturally together. Stories are our relationship. If we as pastors are going to spend our entire lives telling the old, old story, maybe we ought to develop our wit as storytellers. I will deal with adversaries one last time in this series. I know that there are those who would say, "Keep away from stories, teach only precepts. Stories fictionalize great truth." The exact opposite is true. Stories concretize great truth. Stories keep a society sane; they do not lead a society to fictionalize away the truth that they contain. G. K. Chesterton wrote: "There is a notion adrift everywhere that imagination, especially mystical imagination, is dangerous to man's mental balance. . . . Imagination does not breed insanity. Exactly what does breed insanity is reason. Poets do not go mad; . . . chess-players do."[4]

In helping people to imagine, we may actually be helping them to mental health. Still, I want to suggest to you that one very important function is served by the preacher who is out to become the best possible raconteur: He is in the business of helping people relate to each other and their world.

Stories and the Relationship Focus

Stories pull interest into intensity. Stories fuse whole theaters full of persons into such a focus that they all rise as one to their feet in roaring applause. They weep in muffled tears that can be heard from the boxes to the lounge or the balcony. Stories pull the interest of thousands of people until they are truly fused in focused relationship. The stories of our lives are part and parcel of someone else's story, so that any single story welds the whole together.

Now as I consider story, I understand the powerful truth hidden in John Donne: "No man is an island, entire of itself: / Every man is a piece of the continent, a part of the main, . . . / Any man's death diminishes me."[5] There are no independent stories. The very words "Once upon a time" say, "Get ready, we are going to relate."

I think I know what my favorite American singer meant when he said, "For my enemy is dead, a man divine as myself is dead."[6] Was Walt Whitman an egoist? No. I think what he was saying is that he was like a minister, a minister who sang all his life, paralyzed and singing from a wheelchair for the last thirty years of his life. Make no mistake about it, you are from God, unique in who you are. No one else can tell a story quite like you that will fuse your world in oneness.

177

Out in the marvelous Southwest, those wonderful Hopis and Nava-jos have artists who fashion not only pots but here and there a ceramic icon called the Storyteller. Here, clustered against a mammoth terra-cotta squaw, are fifteen or twenty fire-glazed papooses, and the papooses are gathered with rapt attention on the face of the Story-teller. She tells stories; she brings oneness.

Stories, however, can serve as a negative reversal that divides fam-ilies and communities for years. Our Grandpa Young recently died at one hundred two years of age. It was around 1900 that Grandpa first noticed certain liberal trends among Methodists and Campbel-lites, the other two congregations in our community. "In those days," he said, "the Methodists sprinkled and the Campbellites baptized upstream in the Salt Fork River, letting the river current wash the dresses of lady converts high enough to be lewd before the Lord. We Baptists baptized in a more godly manner downstream and thus were more pleasing to the Lord.

"Further, in the '30s," he said, "the liberal Methodist farmers had become the first to work in the field on Sunday, and in the '40s they had dropped evening services. In the early '50s, they had been the first to begin using the new red-covered, communist-inspired Bible." No doubt about it to Grandpa, their story was not the old, old story, for "virgin" in that modernist, communist Bible had been replaced with "young woman," and some Methodists up in Hutchinson, he had heard, no longer sang "Low in the Grave He Lay" on Easter.

If theological homogeneity is important for our story-oneness, so is sociological homogeneity. Peter Wagner of Fuller Seminary is famous for teaching that churches grow by homogeneous units. Most of the time, the preacher storyteller tells only sociological-unit stories.

Where did Jesus find the most abuse and nonacceptance? When he told stories of widened application. For instance, take the para-ble of the son who was killed by the unfaithful vineyard keepers, or the story of the great banquet that was opened to the Gentiles because the Jews who were bidden to the feast would not come. These are examples of stories that are widened beyond the narrow prejudice of the listeners.

Homogeneous communities like stories that are told for their specific community where all the various elements of the stories "fit." So while the anthem of the church may be, "Tell me the old, old story," middle-class suburbanites really sing, "Tell me the old, old, middle-class suburban story."

What are we really doing by picking a suburban Christ for suburbanites? Or a grenade-throwing Christ for liberation theologians? We are giving our particular kind of spiritual community a narrow focus. We are blinding them one eye at a time by ghettoizing. We build provinces by keeping our stories parochial. We must let Christ's story grow wider until it does not engage in parochialism. For just as stories can provincialize, so they may also globalize and awaken consciences.

Christ himself becomes the role model for the preacher as a storyteller. Christ ultimately hung upon a cross because he globalized in a province. Since God is global, every call to preach is a call to see over boundaries, whether they be denominational boundaries or ethnic boundaries or boundaries of mere geography. Seeing widely is ever liberation. Once we have seen, we cannot go back to the province and see our stories as comfortable philosophies that shoe-horn-slipper us into stingy narrowness. There is a world out there, and the great gift every preacher storyteller can give his people is to cause them to see widely.

I have always said that I would love Christ if for no other reason than he was able to take the none-too-cosmopolitan disciples and say, "Your comfortable Galilee is gone now. You are all stewards of the world. Therefore, go! With all of your limitations, speaking with dull Aramaic in the crisp Latin ghettos of Rome, tell the global truths; they are the ones that matter." I do like thinking of Peter, the Galilean fisherman, who found himself so captive to so great a story that he died two thousand miles from the sea after a common carpenter taught him he was responsible for the world.

Yet here is the paradox of our world stories: They must be real within the provinces where they are told, even by those of cosmic mind. The story Peter learned in Galilee must fit the worlds of both Roman senators and slaves. It must hold as much interest in the catacombs as it did along the sandy shores of Galilee. There in tiny, cozy settings, world stories must be heard one at a time, and their application must pull together the local community. For the story is first, last, and always to be relational.

The Story as Happening

Stories, sermons, and relationships all have one other thing in common: They happen. Yet our pulpit stories, which ought to mold and define our communities, have a way of becoming predictable. The greatest of all possible challenges lies within us. How do we tell the same old story every week without it garnering the quality of sameness? When we consider church worship services, it is perhaps a miracle that anyone comes at all, ever. We do keep telling the same old story, and it is a well-defined story throughout the West.

Charismatics have shown us the relational power of happening. I suspect the early success of the charismatic movement may have been spurred on by the heavy liturgy in Episcopal and Lutheran churches. As spontaneity builds relationship, liturgy tends to isolate, often with high-sounding elitist walls of boredom. Pentecostals will crush you in coils of *koinonia*, but in a day of virile loneliness, their churches have exploded in size, proving that most of us would rather risk a little wildfire than have no fire at all. Being relational is a happening in worship. It's Sunday Night Live every week. Heavy liturgy is elitist, allowing us to think well of ourselves, but spontaneity is the soil of the Spirit, making the cold ones warm.

I spoke recently at an interdenominational missionary conference in Latin America. The elitist churches I visited in that country had miles of empty pews with even the hymnals standing upright and separate in the racks. The charismatic churches, however, were crowded. People related to each other in an atmosphere made friendly by mariachis, tambourines, and maracas. There was enthusiasm and warmth there.

Story doesn't work at all without spontaneity. Stories, once told, lose half their interest when they are told a second time. My children used to say, "Daddy, make up a story." The commandment to make up a story points to the most charming aspect of stories—their spontaneity. Life happens, and stories always concern themselves with life; therefore, stories happen.

It is the happening in transcription that makes a story. When a story sounds contrived, it walks with heavy boots and there is no innate joy. When a story comes so fast that it cannot be written down, it dances, and a wondrous intrigue occurs. Winnie the Pooh once testified: "'Poetry and Hums aren't things which you get, they're things which get *you*. And all you can do is go where they can find you. . . . So there it is,' said Pooh, when he had sung this to himself three times. 'It's come different from what I thought it would, but it's come. Now I must go and sing it to Piglet.'"[7]

It is the manner of a story's coming that is unrehearsed and unforced. The story must appear to have come easily, without having to be snatched. Moreover, the telling must seem snuggly and slouch-cushioned. If it gets formal and demanding and austere, it will frighten or be shamed into the contempt we all keep for the hoity-toity. Pooh's last line is the one that so intrigues me. "Now, I *must* go and sing it to Piglet." There is something "musty" in good inspired stories. They must be told and retold.

The Emotion of Relationship

One of the things that occurs immediately in story is relationship. We laugh and cry at stories, and when we are laughing and crying, we allow our common tears or laughter to bind us together.

Emotion is the language of relationship. Small wonder, then, that when some stories are told, the auditor will say, "How touching." We might wonder that they don't say of the story, "How audible," since stories would seem to be more heard than touched. Yet touching is the word, and touching emphasizes the sensual and the relational. We greet stories, not ear first, but skin first, for skin is the stuff of relationship.

Confessional preaching moves the audience spatially toward you until finally your hearts indeed touch. A prominent cable evangelist

181

in the '80s fell in a sexual entanglement that, for a few days, was shrouded in scandal. I had never appreciated his ministry nor listened to his sermons, but when I heard he was going to confess, I thought I would enjoy his confession more than his condemnation, so I tuned in. It was amazing that as he confessed, I found that he closed the distance between us. As he told his story, I moved in closer and closer, almost sorry I couldn't get inside my television set. It was as though he whispered his repentance in my very ear.

Remember, confessional preaching often wars against authority. To tell stories of our lives which embarrass or shock our congregations will leave us feeling overconfessed and underattended. I remember a certain deacon who used to pray publicly, "Lord, hide our preacher behind the cross and let us see only Jesus in him." I don't know how well God answered his prayers since I never have felt very hidden in the pulpit, but rather far too exposed and exhibitionist. Still, I think at the heart of his weekly prayer was the idea that the less obvious the storyteller is, the more potent the story becomes. In that, at least, I am in agreement.

A storyteller who only tells us about dragons is not to be compared with the storyteller whose art erases himself and leaves us alone with the dragon breathing down our necks. Back in Oklahoma, I heard any number of evangelists. One of the hellfire itinerants said on his brochure, "Forty-Eight Hours in Hell." He had died (of what I can't recall) and then been miraculously restored to life. I went to hear this living dead man, whose former rigor mortis had now come to afflict his sermons. There was a certain flare in his return from hell. He had a purple suit and a song leader's haircut. He had a big tent filled with lightbulbs and candleflies. In his sermon, "Forty-Eight Hours in Hell," he drew long and lurid pictures of his death experience. It took him nearly as long to preach on hell as his visit had taken.

On the other hand, here and there among Oklahoma evangelists, I would hear an old parson preach. He would sometimes move in a country defiance of grammar, but, in spite of his polarity to Shakespeare, I soon found myself enthralled. As I listened, the storyteller did seem to hide himself behind the cross, and thus history lived and danced in light.

Conclusion

Our churches at eleven o'clock on Sunday mornings are a tribute to the relational power of story. For whatever congregational grudges there may be, it seems to me that while we tell our story, we all move closer together. Some hear for the first time, and their relationship with Christ is born. Others only feel somehow better about each other. Stories call us to see the things we have in common. In such a commonality of mood, the story lives, and we who listen are fused into oneness. Let none rebuke our togetherness!

Not often enough have I seen people stand at the end of my sermon to say, "The story I heard this morning has intersected my own life story. I weep in brokenness, or in new relationship, or in simply being one with the storyteller." When that has happened, I have laid aside my seminary journals and said to God, "Make us one. Circumstances and the world will do all they can this week to divide us . . . but in the meantime, God, make us one. Fold us up in a warm togetherness and teach us we are more alike than we thought before the story started."

The Story as Salvation

An illustration is like a row of footlights that shed light on what is present on the stage. If you turn the lights on the audience, they blind the people.

Haddon Robinson

If the hearers need teaching, tell the truth by means of narrative.

Aurelius Augustine

I thought the old sun shone a good deal brighter than it ever had before—I thought that it was just smiling upon me; and as I walked out upon Boston Common and heard the birds singing in the trees, I thought they were all singing a song to me. Do you know, I fell in love with the birds. I had never cared for them before. It seemed to me that I was in love with all creation. I had not a bitter feeling against any man, and I was ready to take all men to my heart.

D. L. Moody, after his conversion

In the Rijksmuseum in Amsterdam, I was overwhelmed by the size of Rembrandt's paintings—wall-size, sailcloth canvases depict-

185

ing "The Dutch Masters" and "Nightwatch." As I stood, amazed, talking to the curator, I learned that during the war, before the Germans entered Amsterdam, patrons of the museum took those huge paintings out of their frames, rolled them up like carpets, and sealed them in wax, making them waterproof. A huge art underground was underway. The paintings were moved from culverts to granaries to farms—all to keep the art from falling into enemy hands. Desperation has never been friendly to art. Herein lies our quandary as preachers.

The Christian theology of salvation (soteriology) has always been desperate stuff, defying sermon as craft. The very word *Savior* means "deliverer," and our preachment is as serious as our Savior's last words: "Into all the world, preach the gospel to every creature—lest I should have to say to them some day, 'Depart from me ye cursed into everlasting fire, prepared for the devil and his angels.'"

Our hymns speak to the desperation of our saving message:

> Rescue the perishing,
> Care for the dying,
> Snatch them in pity
> From sin and the grave.

From my youth, I still remember singing another haunting hymn:

> Oh bring your loved ones—
> Bring them to Jesus,
> Bring every brother and sister to him;
> When come the reapers
> Home with the harvest,
> Oh, may your loved ones be safe gathered in.

It seems that the more seriously we take evangelism in preaching, the less important we view the importance of homiletics as a discipline. All Protestants (and most Catholics) reacted to the decadence of the Roman Catholic church during the years between 1470 and 1530. The six popes who reigned during those decades remain at least equal with current televangelist morality. When Protestants feel the need to apologize for the hypocrises of our own day, we have but to remember those six popes to square all apologies and recognize that *all* churchmanship is capable of sin.

Roderigo Borgia's papacy was a time of great decadence. There was little preaching against sin, and the Borgias never held gospel crusades in the Florence arena. In the midst of all this moral decadence, the High Renaissance blossomed across Europe. In little more than a decade after the Borgias, Martin Luther tacked his theses to the Wittenberg church door, and for the next four hundred years, Protestantism grew utterly serious about preaching a desperate gospel. While our current desperation has kept some of the world from going to hell, our interest in the arts has become nearly nonexistent.

Our urgency is so great that many would argue it is pointless to tell our little pulpit stories when so many are lost and hell-bound. What shall we then conclude? Those in the secular world usually see our desperation as quaint. Still, "Jesus saves!" is the cry of the church. His story is one of desperate alternatives—believe or be damned. Like Jonathan Edwards, we step into the pulpit with the clear intention of keeping sinners out of the hands of an angry God, but our sermons must cry "Fire!" in their urgency. That being so, why is the salvation story so often reduced to an exercise in boredom?

Ralph Lewis of Asbury Seminary tells of a young precept preacher who discovered an answer to this question. The student, named Randy, complained that when he preached, the parishioners all looked out the windows of his rural church to watch the cows. The pastor was snuggling his congregation into heavy-eyed boredom until he learned how to illustrate. Randy listened to Dr. Lewis's suggestion that he illustrate his listeners into involvement. The next week, the young pastor fairly bounced into his class, crying out, "Boy, nobody watched the cows this Sunday, . . . I started with this sentence: 'The go-go dancer knocked on the parsonage door on Saturday night.'"[1] Do stories about go-go dancers actually have a place in the sermon? Many city parishioners have found the sermon sleepy even with no window full of cows to sit with them till the plodding benediction should come.

187

Jesus is the great nonfiction epic of the church. Yet faith alone tells us his story is true. We all cry like apostles in anguish, "Lord, I believe. Help thou mine unbelief." While we preach, the congregation wrangles, and the questions fly: Was there a Jesus? Is there a Jesus? Did he die? Is he alive? Where is he now? Will he stay there? Is he coming again? These story matters are crucial to them. For upon this story, they are saved or damned.

Therefore, *soterios* is the hard and fast business of our preachment. Salvation is the *teleios* I talked about in chapter 10. Christianity does not *contain* the story of Christ, it *is* the story of Christ, but it contains our own story as well. As I said earlier, these two stories told at the same time equals our testimony—the personal story we tell *because* we believe it and *until* we believe it. The best testimonies always contain these three realities—grace, the narrow escape, and enlarged reality.

Grace

Grace we define as "unmerited favor," or as our time-worn acrostic declares: God's Riches At Christ's Expense. Simply put, grace is love, and more love than we deserve. Shakespeare is honest about it: "Use every man after his desert, and who shall scape whipping?"[2] Grace always loves the unlovable and gives the rotten kid its best apple.

If grace is such a great miracle, why doesn't everybody lap it up instantly? Grace is a rather demanding miracle that says, "Don't just stand there in the April wind gazing at my bloody hands, 'take up your own cross.'" This grace is the struggle at Peniel, Jacob face-to-face with the pursuing Hound of Heaven. Grace is the great surgeon that dismembers us, amputating self from reputation. Grace confronts us as threatening love and cries, "Disbelieve me if you dare, for I am sometimes the hunter and sometimes the hunted. I am your wounded pursuer, teaching you that crucifixion is contagious. I will dog your emptiness till you bear my stigmata. Then we both shall be bleeding lovers seeking others." Like Captain Ahab, we who receive his grace are "alive, but branded!" Ahab, in his soul's need, flung his cry to sea and wind: "To the last I grapple with thee." So ever do we grapple with grace.

Faith is this glorious grappling with mystery. Why preach this hideous struggle at Peniel? Why not merely thump the gospel in strong demand, till every sinner weeps through the screaming? Grace! Shout it, wail it, moan it, *agonizesthe*! Why must we grace-a-holics go on forever talking about it? Perhaps we do so because grace is a narrative, a tender epic of love. It breathes softly from a cross.

Precepts are austere and rasp harsher truths. They can compound and obscure grace altogether. Too often, precepts get commentary-clotted and so nasal that they wake the crickets in Gethsemane. When all story ceases, grace itself may cease to flow fresh. Christ's saving wounds then may become scabbed over by Greek word studies, and our people watch cows.

Herman Melville's Dr. Cuticle, a white-jacketed authority, performs an appendectomy on a deckhand. The simple sailor is laid out and made ready for surgery. Dr. Cuticle begins his work with precision and incision. He lays knife to abdomen and all is seen, from the liver to the pink-folded passages of life. Cuticle, however, is a showbiz doctor who is fascinated by his own performance. Picking through the viscera of his poor patient, he explains to the crew of the ship the entire interior of the deckhand. The operation is impressive, but by the time Cuticle has sewn up the patient, he has been dead for quite a long while. Dr. Cuticle was so enthusiastic in his exegesis that he hadn't noticed his patient had died.[3] If our pulpit exegesis gets clever with alliterative outlines and spunky word studies that fascinate while our patients die, our preaching fails.

The Narrow Escape

We are all being saved by the skin of our teeth, or, as Paul says, "so as by fire" (1 Cor. 3:15 KJV). In salvation, we escape not only from hell but also from the mundane and joyless present. Joy is the jettison mechanism in a life grown heavy, the answer to all depression, the most infallible proof of the presence of God. Joy often loses to desperation in our sermons. When dealing with the all-important issue of salvation, desperation will only sell when we preachers do not overstate the case. I am ever struck by the fact that more than thirty-five thousand churches in my own denomination continue to talk about sin, death, and hell from week to week. Yet these consistent cries of desperation are met with sparse results at the invitation. The problem, perhaps, is that our desperate words are out of sync with our casual lifestyles. We talk desperation, but it is mostly talk.

We have compounded this problem by institutionalizing the altar call. So often our church services conclude with an invitation, not because the Spirit leads us, but because it is an institutional custom. Some denominations even print forms for church clerks to record any decisions for Christ. In this situation, the respondents might more honestly sing,

> Just as I am without one plea,
> I've come to sign form one-oh-three
> That the church clerk just handed me.
> Oh Lamb of God, I come.

We are filled with revivalistic urgency. "Yes, yes, I see that hand," we say. "Be sincere, even if you don't mean it," we instruct. We still use words of desperation, but we are casual and chatty and institutional and back to kissing babies after each service. We have dulled our credibility edge. We cannot convince the world that we are in the disaster business with such institutionalized desperation. We need either to talk less about hell or believe in it more. Our sermons must be careful not to say more than we really feel. For most of the world, a contrived urgency does not compute.

The very etymology of the word *disaster* calls for integrity. *Disaster* means to be separated (*dis*) from the stars (*aster*). Robert Heinlein, in *Job: A Comedy of Justice,* has his fundamentalist preacher preach about the desperation of the life that is separated from the stars, but Heinlein's preacher is a harsh herald whose trumpet would be better used as a planter for a morning glory. He cries out in his scalding apocalypse: "Hellfire and damnation! Not for just a little while but

190

through all eternity! Not some mystical, allegorical fire. . . . it never stops. Never! . . . For two thousand years sweet Jesus has been begging you, *pleading* with you, to accept Him. . . . So, once you are burning in that fiery Pit . . . don't go whining about how dreadful it hurts."[4] Heinlein's sermon doesn't intrigue me as much as this stirring insight: "Religious ecstasy is the strongest human emotion; when it's there, you can smell it!"[5] Preaching too often on hell is no incentive to repentance. Only where emotional impact and integrity meet can the Spirit do his work.

I have spoken twice earlier on the absolute imperative of integrity. Again, I say that authenticity is gained when both the details and the plots of our pulpit stories are honest. G. K. Chesterton reminds us that we must not allow the grace story to stray too far from what he calls the world of limits: "Art is limitation; the essence of every picture is the frame. If you draw a giraffe, you must draw him with a long neck. If, in your bold creative way, you hold yourself free to draw a giraffe with a short neck, you will really find that you are not free to draw a giraffe." Chesterton concludes by saying, "If a triangle breaks out of its three sides, its life comes to a lamentable end."[6] Neither can we set evangelism free of its desperation and have it remain evangelism. Grace ends when our sermon stories lose their authenticity.

Our stories must contain *pointedness* as well as *authenticity* to motivate others toward the desperate need of being saved. Pointedness means that our stories must not amble—all who hear them must understand them when they are over. They must clearly understand why we told them in the first place. One reason that stories so often fail in preaching is that the preacher tells them only to keep attention, not to direct hearers toward the issues of the sermon. Jokes, therefore, are often sermonic pitfalls. Jokes have a way of making the sermon look like buffoonery and can detract from its pointedness. This is not true, however, of the use of humor as a whole. To learn the art of breaking seriousness by punctuating it with lightness is a gift. Humor can lift heaviness, saying to all, "Let us laugh together so that we do not lose our path through all this seriousness."

Pointedness acknowledges that our listeners do not come to church seeking an answer to their *eternal* lostness. They come more often compelled by some huge burden that is destroying their *temporary* sanity. If they do not get this temporary help, they may soon decide that both preachers and sermons are of little use in the world, promoting the cliché, "People are leaving the churches, having given up on God."

All living needs here-and-now answers. George MacDonald called for the preaching of three grand essentials: someone to love, something to do, something for which they can hope.[7] Our listeners attend our stories in search of these grand essentials.

The preacher's best-attended stories will deal with emotional and financial security. The words *safe* and *saved* pass close. Safety is security, and security is a chief need in this uncertain world where anything can happen. Security pervades every area of our worship, beginning with our hymns.

> "My soul in sad exile was out on life's sea, till I entered the haven of rest . . ."
> "Oh, *safe* to the rock that is higher than I . . ."
> "Under his wings I am safely abiding."

Our fearful natures declare themselves in such images as these. In life as we say in worship hymns, we are hiding from danger and poking our fearful heads out of rocky crevasses or from beneath chicken's wings. However quaint these images seem, security needs ever draw people to church. We might wish that church members came to church to be armed for Christian advancement. But alas, some came to church out of a pressing need to be safe. We pulpit troubadours may lament the fact that the church for many is only a place to hide—a haven from the excessive brutality of life. Here, amid thundering organ pipes and cascading colored glass, we leave the errant evil world of harshness and cruelty and inhumanity. In the safe zone of the nave, we tortoises at last thrust head from shell and sing of meaning. We, the world's abused, have at last come together in a hiding place. There, shut in with Jesus, we most often sing first of safety and later of salvation.

192

Evangelicals frequently put down the popular positivist preachers because they take the pie from the sky and put it on this present earthly table. The reason pulpit positivism succeeds is that it deals with here-and-now security. To offer a narcissistic age all the goodies of life with no crosses is dishonest, but to fail to see the immediate lure of temporal appeal will keep us telling stories that are so futuristic they cannot minister.

It is true that the churches must preach apocalypse, but as Frances Ford Coppola pointed out, the apocalypse is now. Apocalypse always teaches that God is coming, following a purging and vindicating firestorm. The real firestorm, however, is not coming—it is here. Preachers must tell others how to deal with the current fires that consume their poor nervous systems. Only when we extinguish the closer fire will they listen to our talk of the more distant fires of hell. Only those we safely take from the water will sit in leisure to learn our theology of the harbor.

Enlarged Reality

William James saw evangelical Christianity as so intense that it obscured most other values. James, who refused Christian conversion, did so because he said that the truth which should set men free actually imprisons them in narrowness. Once our story gets provincialized, it no longer intersects the world of art, science, and literature as a whole. Thus the truth that should set us free incarcerates us in narrow walls of dogma. I have long argued that grace which so narrows perception is not a particularly good deal. Madeleine L'Engle argued wideness as a virtue of art: "The imaginary work must have such an effect on us that it enlarges our own sense of reality."[8] I would like to take this same stand for grace: Grace must enlarge our sense of reality. The word *yasha,* "salvation" in the Old Testament, means enlargement—to create space, to free by widening. To be saved is not just to be unchained, it is to have the walls of our narrowness moved back until we have ultimate room to understand all our world. Sermons that consistently create *yasha* are rare indeed.

The problem with the Savior's reign in most churches is that his kingdom is one of mere committee meetings and casserole dinners. Jesus grows small in prisons of denominational and institutional egoism. The pulpit must set the Lion of Judah free. We deny him sovereignty when we cage him in little packing boxes of small understanding. Then we do not make our world Christian. We only Christianize it with Christian radio, Christian television, Christian magazines, and Christian loyalties. Fencing ourselves in with such one-dimensional truths, we become the captives of our own intensity.

We must unwall our story. We must give Jesus a bigger throne, a vaster sovereignty. He must be raised on a dais in campus malls and at the frantic computer bazaars of Wall Street. He fears neither the arts nor the sciences. His story must walk widely, and its tellers must be men and women of breadth and depth. Our hypocrisy will then be gone. We *can* change our world. We can be knowing, no longer speaking of world consequence from hot-blooded religious ghettos. Rather, we shall tell the old, old story, having set it against as much of human understanding as we can.

Conclusion

With this studied story, we shall advance on the knowing world. In the wake of Christ's great "Once upon a time," no man or woman will be left the same. Earth will be made better, heaven will be populated by his story, and, glory of glory, we are called to be its tellers. We shall be heralds of hope in a day of cultural desperation, sentinels who reply to the emptiness of our time.

Part 4

Preparation and Delivery

Notes on Preparation

The office of preaching is an arduous task. . . . I have often said that, if I could come down with a good conscience, I would rather be stretched upon a wheel and carry stones than preach one sermon. For anyone who is in this office will always be plagued; and therefore I have often said that the damned devil and not a good man should be a preacher. But we're stuck with it now. . . . If I had known I would not have let myself be drawn into it with twenty-four horses.

Martin Luther

The only thing in God's economy that can ever take the place of preaching is better preaching. And every man is capable of that. Not of good preaching. Good preaching may be quite beyond us. But better preaching. That is beyond none of us.

Paul E. Scherer

> He spoke of lilies, vines and corn,
> The sparrow and the raven;
> And words so natural yet so wise
> Were on men's hearts engraven.
> And yeast and bread and flax and cloth
> And eggs and fish and candles—
> See how the most familiar world
> He most divinely handles.

Tyrrell Green

The question I posed in the introduction, I raise this final time: Can preaching really be taught? Joseph Sittler answered: "Disciplines correlative to preaching can be taught, but preaching as an act of witness cannot be taught."[1] For the parts of preaching that can be taught, I offer this section.

The preparation of sermons sometimes seems to be a fading art. Why? Perhaps the hyperdrive emotionalism that characterizes cable television (and some mass evangelism) has championed a gooey new relationship that offers only chummy togetherness rather than a true altar encounter. The real culprit, however, may be a widespread and deplorable lack of sermon preparation.

The communicator's mind is altogether important. John Calvin wrote, "All preaching, true and sound preaching, consists of two parts: the knowledge of God and of ourselves."[2] Communication can never surpass in quality the mind from which it comes. The preparation of sermons does not begin on Monday morning (or Saturday night) when the preacher sits down to examine a text. Sermon preparation has too many facets to be examined in a chapter of this size, but the communicator must fix in his mind one principle: The twenty- or thirty-minute homily must remain instructive, cogent, and life changing. The enormity of this responsibility means that it requires a great deal of study time. Homer Buerlein records that "Harry Emerson Fosdick spent one hour in study for each minute of his sermon."[3] Studied preaching understands that it is neither godly nor ethical to hold people's minds for any length of time without nourishing them.

Life Preparation

Total Person, Total World

Sermons begin in the center of our schedules, our world, our very lives. This is what we earlier called the preaching habitat. Sermons are about the Bible, about God, about living, and they represent the distillation of all we know and have seen as we bring that knowledge and experience to bear upon some passage of Scripture. As we marry

198

our experience to the study of Scripture, we ever ask, "Why is this double light of text and experience so important to those who listen, and, above all, why is it important right now?"

If Flannery O'Connor can allege that a good writer writes about the whole world, then surely a good preacher preaches about the whole world. The preacher thus becomes a world interpreter. He is not just interpreting the Scriptures, he is centering on all of life. On behalf of his listeners, he is trying to make all the pieces of hurt, anguish, debt, struggle, joy, eternity, the six great land masses, political reform, revolution, health, art, science, and philosophy all fit together in such a way that those who hear him can honestly say, "His words touch all of life. They make sense."

Naturally, if a preacher is going to make the universe fit in his study, both his preaching and his worldview are important. Parochialism sells only narrowly; it is nearsighted. It hasn't tested its theories far enough, nor seen enough of the sun to describe the light. Provincialism may succeed for a while, but only in a province. Ultimately it has no great answers.

So the very first step of preparing sermons is not the consideration for specific study. Laying out the commentaries is not where the best sermons begin. The first step in sermon preparation is the preacher's willingness to know widely, to live and walk with his eyes open through life. His world is big, beckoning sermons to be big.

Testimonial Preaching

Having studied David Buttrick's masterpiece, *Homiletics*, I must stress its importance as a work to be read and understood. His book, however, falls short in failing to see the importance of testimony in preaching. Sermons should be about the world and life. On the one hand, Buttrick counsels his readers to seldom use personal illustrations, for they distract the listener's mind from the real subject of the sermon by placing the focus on the preacher. On the other hand, I am altogether convinced that sermons are not only about people, but delivered by people.

199

Keeping this in mind, I believe that a part of our preparation should be to observe people and to include within our sermons the elements of this observation. This kind of preaching is called testimony. If one needs evidence of this, Paul gives his testimony as part of his sermons at least three times in the New Testament. Testimony causes people in the pews to move in and to see how the speaker has lived through all that is being discussed. Surely personal integrity must be a part of every preacher who prepares to preach by asking, "How am I handling the truths that I am asking my hearers to believe or to endorse?" This same question will be filling the minds of the people as they listen. "Do you, Reverend, practice what you preach? Give us some personal testimony that what you're saying will, indeed, work for us." A consistent diet of preaching that never contains personal experience always lacks authority.

Insight by Polarity

In preparing sermons it is important to be sure your preparation deals with living contrasts. Two contrasts that must not escape good preparation are the experiential/academic and the observational/existential.

Experiential/academic. Sermon preparation that does not contrast these two values cannot be appropriated by the listeners. Books are fine, and a book quoted in a sermon will often connote authority, but authority alone comes off as bossy or know-it-all. The other side of quoting is experience: "While this book says this, I have found . . ." or, "This writer may be right about this, but here's what I discovered one day . . ."

Sermon preparation must take care to balance these polarities. This is true even when quoting the Bible. People generally welcome biblical authority, but many of the Bible's admonitions are severe and remote. They need to be brought home by the analysis of personal experience. A pastor friend of mine told me he always had trouble understanding how God could be both the lover and judge of humanity, until one day his good friend who was a judge became his arbiter at traffic court. When his good friend fined him for a traffic misdemeanor, the academic, theological truth became experience. In similar ways, our preparation must make the academic accessible through experience. Authority and practicality can then become friends.

Observational/existential. Sermons must be prepared when the light is good. We must be able to see clearly all that we talk about. To prepare a sermon with fuzzy vision is to communicate only fuzzy truths. Seeing and describing do not make a sermon rich. Observation must be evaluated existentially, in terms of its meaning to our lives. Observation says, "Here's how I see it." Existentialism cries, "Ah, yes. But here's how I lived through it!" If you object that these things do not belong in a book on the preparation of sermons, remember, if we do not prepare our sermons in the process of living, our sermons will not be living documents.

Life as University

In my first rural parish, most of my flock were suspicious of me because I was in school and seemed bent on getting an education, which, as they saw it, would only make me a book-learning preacher. Their heroes in the pulpit, so they told me, were men like "Ole Beck." Ole Beck was really Pastor Becker, who had never gotten uppity on books and could always find time to ride around a 160-acre furrow on their tractors to "tell 'em how the good Lord made the wheat grow."

I have never tried to pattern my whole life after Ole Beck, but this much I did determine: I would live and preach in context. For these rural saints, this meant that my sermons might hurry past their literary excellence in favor of relationship, but it also meant that I would see life as a university. If I wanted to serve a delicious Sunday meal, then my sermons needed to gather truths and insights from all of life.

Scripture as Basic

I have not waited to put Scripture farther down on my list of sermon preparation pointers because I see Scripture as a lower priority. Scripture must be more than a sermonic resource from which we draw three points for the hungry crowd. Life preparation of sermons means that we do not go to the Scriptures for sermons. We rather live in the Scriptures from day to day as a part of our life preparation to preach. A pastor who lives in Scripture will have such a ready mind for preaching that the richness of the Bible will erupt into his sermons. Bible words, memorized long ago and close at hand, will abound in his sermons, enriching the hearers as they earlier enriched the speaker. Probably the greatest weakness of preachers is that they only go to the Scriptures for sermons and sermon ideas. How much richer preaching becomes when the pastor sees the Bible as the source of his relationship with God and owns a constant hunger for God from which sermons can draw power. The preacher who learns to live with the Bible enriching his very existence will preach it in a vital way.

Long-Term Preparation

Buying the Bank

I once heard it said that preachers who change churches every twenty-eight months were moving from pulpit to pulpit because they ran out of pulpit stuff. I know the pressure, but the answer is not to keep going with minimal reserves; we should buy the bank so we always have a pulpit reserve. Long-term study habits and filing systems are the only way to buy the bank. Before I even begin to suggest how this is to be done, I need to say that every pastor must declare himself a student. He must let his congregation know with some force that, while he is open to interruptions—after all, the greatness of a pastor's life comes in his interruptions—he must have study time, and his congregation must honor his demand. Every pastor needs to inform his congregation of his study schedule so that all can join him in protecting his study, for their sake as well as his.

Granting and protecting our study time is the enclosure, but how shall we fill it? I propose that pastors by nature must know how to gather and save. Gathering is done in reading great books and jour-

202

nals and engaging in quality life experience. The books and journals can be annotated, clipped, and filed, but just how is this all done?

Consider books first. When a good insight or illustration occurs in a book, it can be annotated by page number in the flyleaf or in the back of the book. The illustration can be typed onto an index card or half-sheet of paper for filing. Once a month or so these sheets can be filed according to the subjects that will make them easier to recall and use in specific parts of particular sermons.

How is the filing to be arranged? In my case, I arrange them into twenty-eight file folders, beginning with "Apologetics" and progressing through to "Witnessing." In between these two subjects, there are file folders entitled, "Jesus," "Commitment," "Psychology and Sex," and so on. I have generous files of "Family" illustrations, a file on "The Holy Spirit," and one on "Preaching, Writing, and Speaking." Of course, in a strong reading and gathering program, the files will need to be thinned once a year or so, just to be sure that we are not keeping too much material. A file that is too thick eventually becomes useless. Sorting through intimidating volumes of illustrations—most of which will never be used—stops the will.

Ordinarily, the files are the bank, and we own it. In looking over the sermon outline, a file category will suggest itself, and we may turn immediately to this clip file and pull out something pertinent as an illustration or statistic that fits the content and movement of the sermon perfectly. The file also provides enough pertinent material that it is easier to preach with illustrations that don't have to be bent to make them work.

In addition to the bank file, I keep a hodge-podge folder that includes some really poignant stuff. This little folder doesn't have much in it, but everything there is homiletic napalm—so intense it might be worth a little bending to use in an outline. These potent illustrations don't last long, because they are just too good to lay around in a file. Therefore, this folder is my first resource in short-term preparation.

I also keep a book that I use to note practical experiences. I am no longer as faithful in keeping this journal, but if some life experience is good sermon fodder, I write it down and try to make it serve in ways that filed illustrations cannot.

One source of preservation that is usually rewarding is the dismembering and salvaging of old sermons. I rarely throw out an entire sermon. Some part of it can be transplanted from its ailing, useless parent and saved for later graft work on new sermons. I keep worthy illustrations in the "napalm" file, being careful that the previously used illustration was used so long ago that its impact is not diluted.

A final element of gathering is movie, television, or theater quotes and quips. Manuscripts from plays can usually be obtained and read so that the material quoted can be performed correctly. Lines and poems from musicals are available on records and tapes. In movies, I have often jotted a line on my popcorn sack, scrawling it in the dark so that I may later use an advantageous line. All of these things will add to the garnering and strengthening process.

The Annual View

I recommend an annual view of sermon preparation, which means that the pastor should take a block of time during the year to plan his preaching for the next fifty-two Sundays. My annual sermon planning time comes usually in the week between Christmas and New Year's. I take the calendar, type off the fifty-two Sundays of the coming year by date, and begin to fill in the blanks with my sermon title, text, and outline for those Sundays.

First I mark out the Sundays that I will be gone. I am gone about four Sundays throughout the year for vacation or conferences. Then I mark out those special Sundays when I will be preaching on seasonal subjects—for instance, Palm Sunday, Easter, Whitsunday, the four Sundays of Advent, and Thanksgiving. These sermons require preparation, too, but the preparation they require is so seasonal and specialized that I do not try to deal with their preparation the same way I do the other sermons. Then I mark out the Sundays when we will be having a special speaker or an emphasis that will not require me to be in the pulpit. I know all of these dates and speakers at least a year ahead of time. All of these Sundays—vacation, conferences, special and seasonal sermons—will usually take fifteen or sixteen of my Sunday morning sermon times.

Finally, I begin to plan the other thirty-six or so morning sermons. During this planning week I try to outline (and *only* outline) and "textify" these sermons. I then place them in a file folder so that I can look back over them as I plan my year of preaching. Through the successive weeks of the year, I repeatedly refer to this file, gather illustrations to place in each of the separate file folders, and augment the sermon's content between the time of its first outlining and its actual preaching.

Do I preach all of the sermons I plan? No. Within the framework of the year, many things will change. I have even been known to be sick a Sunday here and there. While I am not able to preach all that I had planned, the one-year plan keeps me on track as I direct the spiritual growth of the church. Sometimes I have felt like my long-range preaching plan was not well thought through and find I must scrap a portion of it midyear and substitute something else. Overall, my long-range planning directs my year.

The Series View

I am not a lectionary preacher. I honor, however, any plan that directs a congregation through a systematic study of the whole Bible, for I do believe in series preaching. One of the great things about the oral-exegesis sermons discussed earlier in this book is that oral-exegesis preachers are inevitably series preachers. My suspicion is that what their sermons may lack in original thinking, they will make up in connectedness. Connectedness is a great gift, both for the preacher and the listener. When sermons are connected, preparation gains focus and the disjunctive weeks are tied together as the preacher preaches his way through the year. The series may be exegetical (one year I preached a ten-part series based on the Thessalonian letters), or it may be topical (another year I preached a six-part series on understanding yourself). In a recent thirteen-sermon series on leadership, I drew all the evidences of leadership—networking, vision, delegating, structuring, self-perception, goals, coping with difficult people—

from the life of David. I mention this latter series to say that even if we are preaching topically, the series must be firmly tied in an expositional way to Scripture.

The Spiritual Growth of the Whole Church

Long-term preparation best serves the whole church. Only this kind of preparation remembers the special subgroups within the congregation—the elderly, the youth, the singles, the hurting, the executives. The preparer always asks, "What are these special needs, and what can be done to meet those needs during the coming fifty-two sermons?" Some of those needs will be major enough that whole sermons can be directed to them. Even the smaller needs deserve at least some sermonic consideration, if not a whole sermon.

Short-Term Preparation

Let's walk through a short-term (Sunday to Sunday) preparation guide. On Monday morning, the preacher should review the previous sermon. Whether it is the concluding sermon in a series or a single sermon unrelated to the coming week's text, it is important to look it over. By doing this, the preacher can fix in the mind what was dealt with in the last sermon before the next sermon is prepared. Once I have reviewed the sermon, I edit it one last time and give it to my secretary for reprocessing. I find this allows me to polish the sermon before it is filed for future reference; it provides an excellent review as well. It usually takes about an hour and a half to do this, but it is time well spent.

After the Monday morning review, the text can be set for the coming week's sermon. In my case I would take my one-year planning guide and examine the text to be sure it is appropriate. The preacher who does not prepare long-range should use Monday mornings to select a text and outline it. Those who do practice long-term preparation may already have outlined the text. Still, every outline prepared so far ahead of time may need revision.

206

On Tuesday through Friday, the daily sermon preparation time should augment the outline with illustrations, related Scriptures, and the introduction and conclusion. Perhaps a full sermon manuscript will develop during these four days. Take care, however, that the sermon not be so written that its extemporaneous character is jeopardized. Writing as much as time permits allows the preacher to polish the ideas and phrases he wants to hold in mental readiness. Writing ever stretches ideas, improves phraseology, links logic, and helps the preacher to own the sermon. Further, writing lets the preacher speak clearly with fewer temptations to chase rabbits in the pursuit of the spoor. By Friday evening, the content should be set.

I will look at structuring and outlining next, but no two sermons should be outlined alike. Certainly, no two preachers should ever try to go about it in the same way. Preparation and delivery should be as unique as preachers themselves. David Buttrick in *Homiletics* organizes all sermon preparation around moves and structures. He wisely counsels, "To produce a sermon, we will first need to construct a basic, stripped-down structural design. Scripture passages produce different fields of understanding, and therefore, demand different basic designs; there are *no* stock patterns into which meaning can invariably be stuffed."[4] A sufficient word to the homiletically wise.

In outlining, rigidness must be avoided. To say every sermon should have three points is like saying every day should have three acts, every book ten chapters. Sermon design should see logic and reason blended in the direction that the preacher wishes his argument to go. Three-part outlining has some merit in that it is a familiar sermon form and listeners may find its familiarity comfortable. Remember, however, that every great sermon has only one point. There may be three steps in the move to convince, there may be five, but there is one point.

Two mornings of sermon preparation remain. Saturday morning the outline should be reviewed one last time. Severe sermon scrutiny is Saturday's stuff. Look for and repair woodenness, silliness, shallowness, and redundancies. If so little of the sermon is left after this repair that it won't fill a twenty-minute Sunday slot, last-minute prosthetics may have to replace the amputations. When the sermon is thoroughly edited, the preacher must try to memorize the key points and subpoints before leaving his study.

Sunday mornings should find the pastor in his study early. This is a crucial time for me when I seek to devotionalize my sermon in my own eyes. I realize my congregation does not want a treatise; they want a sermon. They conceive the sermon to be the Word of God from a man of God. Since much of the week's preparation has been academic, I now want to arrive at a frame of heart that will reflect my ambassadorial status before God. At this point, I have to admit that some of my sermon preparation has been more a matter of scholarship than devotion. In the final hours before I preach, I pray, retype some of my thoughts, and seek to incarnate Christ for the coming delivery. I have even scrapped whole sermons during this time because I felt they were wooden and void of Christ. I would, for my part, rather extemporize with no preparation than preach an oration that contains the structure of good delivery but is empty of Spirit.

The sermon should remain in process right up to the time it is preached. In a real sense, no sermon is ever finished and then laid aside till the preaching time. The best sermons may undergo some rearranging of thought or illustration even during the offertory. I don't think I have ever completely finished a sermon in thirty years of preaching. I always feel with more time I might have improved them, but I must preach them because, after all, it is Sunday and their time has come. I am an artist and have had a similar difficulty saying that a painting is finished. I have decided that a painting is complete when I am willing to live with it, not when I could not dab it with a bit more color. A sermon, too, never gets so prepared that no more refining is possible. When the preacher can live with its content and movement and integrity, the homily is ready to be preached.

The final act of Sunday morning preparation for me is what I call breaking. Breaking is the act by which I stop the cathexis I have been building with my sermon all week. Breaking means I quit praying, either alone, with the deacons, or with other interested prayer partners. I leave my study and mix with or "tangibilitate" (as Father Divine used to say) with the people as they gather in the halls and the foyer of the church. I talk with them, try to feel the burdens they bring to church or have been carrying through life. I laugh, confer, and try to become one of them. Breaking is, in a sense, incarnational—the step of becoming human. Breaking keeps me from taking myself too seriously. It enables me to laugh at myself when I make a mistake, even in front of those who come to hear my pronouncements. I have learned that trying to walk out of my study as a thoroughly "prayed-up" saint or "God expert" can only result in phony preaching and, ultimately, bogus humanity. I want to be sure that my attachment to my sermon subject does not render me a pulpit Caesar or a melodramatic, strutting evangelist. In such histrionics, the conversational being of the sermon is lost. I still believe that preachers are better heard week to week and year to year if they maintain something of Ole Beck in the way they relate.

Gathering the Sermon

This last element of preparation I call gathering the sermon. From preacher to preacher the procedures of gathering will vary. For me, there are five things at the center of the gathering process. If I assign them a time of the week, most of the work of gathering the sermon occurs Tuesday through Friday.

Practicing Quotes and Reviewing Memory Work

A preacher should never just read a poem or a paragraph of any other work in his sermons. The preacher is an oral interpreter who should practice every quote and review all memory work, being sure that quotes rise with force and drama. This means that the shorter quotes should be memorized and the long ones should be held so well in mind that they can be delivered with force. The preacher should watch himself preaching. This is particularly important in working with literary quotes. Our services are televised (and taped), but I seldom review myself on videotape. The form I use most frequently is to practice in front of a mirror. I use this method because the mirror is readily accessible and no one has to be there to help me

209

run the equipment. In all my years of preaching, I do not believe that I have ever preached a sermon when I did not review my memory work in this way.

Rehearsing Special Phraseology

Flavor is added to a sermon when its written phraseology is preserved as a part of the oral event. I am always careful not to memorize all of the sermon. The power of certain combinations of memorized words will preserve a sense of excellence. The trick is to keep the memorized part of the sermon flowing easily with the extemporaneous parts. With a little work, smoothness can be achieved.

Marking the Outline

The whole idea of having an outline is to keep the preacher from being tied to the manuscript. The outline should therefore be used only to focus the presentation and not be so detailed as to require constant referral. The preacher must appear free in the pulpit. My outlines are never more than four typed pages and are trimmed in such a way that they fit neatly inside the pages of my Bible. I do this for two reasons. First, I don't use a pulpit, and therefore my Bible is my only prop. Second, I want my outline to be so inconspicuous that I appear to use no notes at all.

Still, the outline should be marked and highlighted so that certain words can be picked up at a glance. The highlighted phrases can quickly suggest whole paragraphs of the sermon. The sermon is a series of points of significance, set to maintain flow. I discovered the value of notching mini-moves in my outline long ago. I generally preach one point of significance per minute. A point of significance may be an illustration, a set of statistics, or a paragraph of strong logic. So my final act of marking my outline is to take a bright red pen and notch the moves by number. Twenty of these mini-moves require twenty minutes. These twenty or so moves comprise the guts of my sermon. I do not want to leave out a single one. In marking my outline for the final time, I make sure each of these points of signif-

210

icance is clearly identified. This ensures that I will not preach past them and lose them.

Extenders and Clippers

There are two categories of points of significance. The first type are less important and can be deleted during the preaching if I need to shorten the sermon. If so, I mentally note and perhaps bracket these in the outline. Such points of significance are really clippers and extenders. Many might refer to these as fillers. They hold interest and are related to the theme, but they are not as necessary to the sense of the sermon as the more crucial points of significance.

Why have extenders and clippers at all? For one thing, the sermon must have a significant length. A sermon that is overly brief will not allow sufficient time for the listener to move with the sermon's logic to its conclusion. I believe this is especially important for sermons that end in a call to altar decision. Unevangelized hearers cannot leave a secular lifestyle too quickly. They must have time to catch hold of the world of Scripture, come out of their mental entanglements, and consider the challenge at hand. Few, if any, great revivals have been based on ten-minute sermons.

Most people rarely make decisions after sermons that are merely intense; they must have participated in some way. Clippers and extenders are best used as interest hooks that invite participation. The point at which the listener's interest begins to flag is the perfect time to insert an extender to be sure that they are still involved. Once the listeners fully shut down, it is nearly impossible to get them back.

The Altar Call

For those whose sermons end in a call for public decision, the sermon must focus on the altar. To preach for decision means the conclusion of the sermon must oversee the entire preparation. The sermon is not there on its own behalf, it exists to call, beckon, transform, and challenge. The call for decision will be central in the preacher's spiritual preparation. Without the pastor's contemplative life being fully in place, the invitation will be neither evocative nor productive. Wooden sermons from wooden lives can result only in wooden altar calls.

I am fully aware now that so many of the church growth technicians are encouraging churches away from the altar call. They say, "Invitations and altar calls intimidate," and are therefore a barrier to church growth. However, church growth is not the primary calling of the church. The church is to preach the demand of God, and if growth occurs, fine. We are not free, however, to emasculate the challenge of the gospel just to preach to more people. For my part, I am convinced the biblical preaching itself can and should confront and call for change in the listener and his or her world from time to time. When the spirit of the altar call is completely gone from Christianity, the faith will be short-lived.

When anyone reacts to the invitation because it is melodramatic and coercive, I understand what the church growth technicians mean. How often have Dixie evangelists shamed, cajoled, and pistol-whipped congregations into psychological defilement. It is time for the church to call a halt to medicine-show religion. This does not mean that invitations as evangelist Billy Graham might give them should stop being the logical conclusion to well thought-out confrontation. Well-planned conclusions, added to well-planned sermons, have historically been the force that calls the world to Christ.

14

Notes on Delivery

If the preacher's going to read it, it's better to give me a copy and save us both time.

Homer K. Buerlein

It doesn't mean Anthony Trollope is correct when he said that "there is, perhaps, no greater hardship at present afflicted on mankind in civilized and free countries than the necessity of listening to sermons."

Edward F. Markquart

A lecture about food is not a steak dinner. Nor is a lecture about the Gospel the same as a proclamation of the Gospel. . . . I don't want lectures instead of sermons. When I am hungry, I want a meal, not a menu or a page from a cookbook.

Lowell O. Erdahl

The method of sermon delivery is a varied and vital study. Preaching, however, is a form of communicating, and sermons must follow the same general rules of good communication as any other form of public speaking.

The Psychology of Delivery

The psychology of sermon delivery should keep three things in mind: identity (who the preacher is and how he is alike or different from the flock), motivation (the preacher is trying to get his listeners to believe in or live the godly life), emotion (none of us can listen free of feeling at the deepest levels of our being).

Identity

All public speaking works best when the hearers feel that the speaker and themselves are alike. Church members frequently sum up their feelings about their pastor by saying, "He's a regular guy." This again is the Ole Beck syndrome. People listen best to someone with whom they feel they have something in common. From this viewpoint, a guest minister may speak not only with greater interest, but with greater freedom than the local pastor. The local pastor cannot speak as one coming to the community of faith, but rather as one who is part of that community. No form of talking down or insinuated rebuke will be tolerated long from him. The pastor is a peer, not an unquestionable authority.

The speaker-hearer identity falls into one of three categories. First, every sermon must face this identity in terms of faith and doctrine. When I hear the word *Republican,* I feel an immediate sense of attachment to anyone who holds that political affiliation. When I hear of anyone who believes in the principles of free education, again a responsive chord is touched. All of us like people who hold those things dear that we hold dear. An identity rises between those whose theological tenets are the same. Some may state proudly, "I am a Methodist, like my father and grandfather before me!" What they mean is that they take great pride in their belief system. Thus a preacher, standing to speak to his congregation, will convey both relationship and identity as he emphasizes the common beliefs of the church. The same things can be said for faith in areas of identity. When we tell others how we feel about God, we reach out to inner relationships.

214

Second, when the preacher discloses what he really needs to be a complete individual, he reaches out to the inner search in every life. Most people have a set of needs that they rarely vocalize. It is this inner need for identity that makes confessional preaching so desirable.

Third, most of us identify with origins. We believe that where we have come from and where we are going, both in life and eternity, contribute to our sense of being fully human. When we find anyone who cherishes our views of origin and destiny, we move psychologically close to that person. The times of greatest bond between myself and my congregation are those very painful times when a beloved church member has died and together we rehearse our commonly held views of eternity.

Motivation

Delivery motivates faith and godly living. Motivation is most effective when it is altruistic. People listen to motivational pitches only when they feel that they are being motivated to do something for God or, perhaps, for themselves. Unfortunately, people give no attention to preachers in business for themselves.

What better illustration of this truth than the fates of certain television preachers who have fallen into national disrepute? It became obvious to viewers that they had become self-indulgent. On the other hand, Christianity's most vital eras are those seasons of history when the church and its spokespersons clearly motivated others to serve God for God's sake. We all want to be motivated to dream a great dream and hold a liberating vision. We feel cheated when we are deceived by preachers who shortstop the great purposes of God with their own agendas.

Emotion

Emotion is the great relater. We love people who we feel are human enough "to feel with." How often the Scriptures say of Christ that he was moved with compassion. When a speaker has lived where we live and hurt as we have hurt, we feel a sense of relationship. Preach-

215

ers whose suffering has made them wise become sources of great understanding.

Sermon delivery that touches our heartstrings with laughter or tears must not be ringmaster stuff, however. We don't want to be entertained by emotion. Emotion is the language of the soul under either stress or buoyancy. A preacher who talks too much of his own stress or buoyancy will find many eager to attend his pilgrimage rather than his sermon. The pilgrimage elicits the weeping or the laughter; the sermon is but part of the pilgrimage.

The Integrity of Delivery

The integrity of delivery always respects four statements: "I am what I appear to be," "I trust you to choose for yourself," "I respect your dignity and worth," and "I appreciate your attendance at my sermon and this church." In each of these issues, the preacher gives credence to the truth.

The preacher must be what he appears. Authenticity cannot be faked; obvious phonies are never heard. Authenticity, like pulpit identity, is learned in pilgrimage. Those who walk in authenticity can preach no other way.

The sense of respect between preacher and listener is the quality of motivation that may be the hardest to come by. When we think we see the best possible course for others to take, it is hard for us to stand by while they make what we believe to be wrong decisions. As a Christian, I am utterly convinced that to refuse to receive Christ is ruin. Believing as I do, I have been most reluctant to see people reject the only possible hope there is. Still, I have had to learn that when it comes to preaching, the glory of the sermon must be that it only presents options, it never precludes them. What others reject as folly, I must allow, even if I see it as wisdom.

The same thing must be true of the pastor as he watches others choose wrong moral codes. Often when I have seen people embrace a lifestyle out of sync with my own, I have had to remind myself that everyone must be free to choose. If my sermons become coercive, listeners point out my coercion in their scoffing disinterest or contempt.

Not much needs to be said here about an individual's God-given dignity and worth. The words *imago Dei* lay at the heart of our gospel. Everybody has worth to God, and from that God-given worth comes dignity. Railing on sin can look like contempt for the sinner. The failure to give dignity to those whom the gospel addresses will cut us off from society and lay waste our proclamation. In a day like ours when psychology, sociology, and anthropology have agreed on the right to dignity, we must not allow social prejudice or spiritual contempt to exist in our lives or sermons. Inherent dignity is a dignity not earned by condescending toward anyone's view or social status.

Western culture probably stands at the apex of all cultures in utter respect for civil rights. Most pastors are doing better than their forebearers in not telling dialect or ethnic sermon stories, but there are still two important areas where our preaching sins. First and foremost, there is still much of a sexist tone in evangelical and fundamentalist pulpits. It makes little difference that we insist that the Bible lobbies for the man being "lord of the home." Since that idea finds no friends in the culture, the pastor who insists on sexist language will also ultimately find antagonism toward his sermons.

A second issue that must be deleted from our sermons is anti-Semitism. Popular novels and post–World War II decorum will not tolerate any hint of this. There exists enough pejorative use of the word "Jews" (especially in the fourth Gospel) that this tone is difficult to avoid, but popular talk shows reflect great resistance toward any insinuation that Jews don't go to heaven or that Christ alone is Savior. My own belief that there is salvation only in Christ makes it mandatory that I do all I can to keep from needlessly alienating my listeners. These listeners are *not* Jewish, but they carry strong feelings about any degree of anti-Semitism.

Needless to say, any slur on cults or bogus, unorthodox Christianity should be avoided in large worship gatherings. To slight Mormons, Jehovah's Witnesses, Moonies, or others by name will alienate. In smaller, tighter (unbroadcasted) sermons, where *all* present are church members, more explicit teachings may be done, not to slur but merely to instruct the church in matters of correct doctrine.

I often tell people, "Thank you for being here today," at the back door. I am aware that they might have stayed home or attended another church. I want a spirit of appreciation to mark my sermons. Even as I deliver them, I will be far less likely to rebuke others if I remember that they have given me a rather priceless gift—time from their busy lives. When I exude honest appreciation, not a groveling for their attention, I find that such affirmation prefaces further friendship.

The Process of Delivery

Eye-to-Eye and Heart-to-Heart Delivery

The process of delivery is too manifold to do much with it here, but before anything else, the delivery must be eye to eye and heart to heart. We have already mentioned both of these ideas in precept. Eye-to-eye means that while we preach, we look into people's eyes. This probably needs to be said, even though it seems elementary. Many preachers look over the heads of their listeners in a kind of fake eye contact that really shuts out the audience. One such preacher to whom I listened confided afterward that he found it much easier "to look 'just over their heads' than to look into their eyes." Nonetheless, it was clear to all present that he was having a conversation with the back wall and not them. He would never have held a personal conversation that way. Why then would he elect to preach in such a cold and affected manner? Eye must meet eye and heart must meet heart for real emotional encounter to occur.

Rules for Good Communication

To help facilitate this encounter, a preacher can follow the general rules for good communication. Four principles should be kept in focus to aid in the process of delivery.

218

Balancing personal distractions with professionalism. Through reviewing videotapes of our sermons, we can be made aware of personal habits that are distracting to our audience. Every church member has heard preachers whose affectations pulled their ears away. These distractions can become embarrassingly amusing—a nervous clearing of the throat, a nomadic moving around the pulpit, an incessant adjusting of eyeglasses. Almost all of these offenses can be eliminated from a pulpit style, but changing any of them requires a concerted effort.

Professionals eliminate anything from the delivery that appears untrained or lacking in dignity. Even personal devaluations that may attract attention must be addressed. During the Watergate hearings, Sam Ervin always referred to himself as a country lawyer. It was a warm self-reference because it was diminutive, but it was belittling to himself. I have heard preachers refer to themselves as poor country preachers in an effort to build relationships by denigrating themselves. This is a poor effort and becomes a personal distraction that steals authority from delivery.

Balancing energy and content. Energy in delivery is important. Too much energy, however, can send the preacher pacing about and gesturing wildly; hyperathletic delivery can be an indication that the content is weak. Energy and content must be kept in balance. Select an energy level that rivets attention while it keeps movement from distracting. Further, exaggerated energy in delivery may cause the preacher to harangue for the duration of the sermon. This causes listeners to feel as though the pastor is speaking down to them. Such energy translates as dogmatism. There may have been a day for dogmatism in preaching, but today isn't it. Our entire culture exists in a relational framework now. Authoritarianism is out. If the preacher's personal energy level translates as authoritarian, this quality of the delivery must be eliminated from the sermon.

Opening, closing, and titling. An introduction is like a porch on a house—the porch must fit the house. An inordinately grand porch will overfit the sermon. If the introduction is the front porch, then the conclusion is the back. Back porches should also not overfit the sermon. They should be short, quickly rehearsing the point of the sermon in a rapid retracing of the logic that leads to the closing.

Remember, the last words of a sermon are the most memorable, so they should be given the most attention. The final story, poem, or challenge should be clearly related to the subject, for at the zero hour any slight digression will confuse.

Concerning the title, clever practicality is best. Ronald Allen suggests these guidelines: Titles should be brief, related to the theme, provocative, composed of a strong image that will start to unlock the minds of the hearers, and be positively stated. He goes on to offer the following examples of strong titles from various well-known expositors:

"Praying through Clenched Teeth" (Fred Craddock)
"God within the Shadows" (Eugene Brice)
"And How Does It All End?" (Edmund Steimle)
"News from Another Network" (David H. C. Read)
"The God Who Came in Out of the Cold" (William Mehl)
"Journey in Search of a Soul" (Frederick Buechner)[1]

Homily versus oration. The psychological revolution has left a wonderful seedbed in which good homiletics can sprout. Delivery should instruct and inspire, but the root meaning of *homiletics* is "talk" or "conversation." Just as the *koine* Scriptures were written in street Greek, the homily was designed to be spoken in the language of the people.

I wrote an article entitled "Preaching in the Vulgate." The import of that article was that if God stepped down from using classical Greek and Latin in the Scriptures, maybe we ought not to consider our pulpit calling to be overly Oxfordian. It is important to remember that while Jesus did not embarrass an audience with poor diction or grammar, he also did not champion a snob religion to appeal to the ultra-educated with gilded lectures. He spoke clearly and simply as he called the world to salvation and life.

Let us also note that Jesus spoke concretely. Every concrete sermon invites attention. Abstract statements only cause the mind to drift away hungrily, with the hearers wishing they were as mystically advanced as the speaker. We must study Christ's teachings until we

220

believe that his concrete, earthly sermons were in part the reason for his authority.

His calling is ours. He is the model for our preaching. His sermons reasoned, beckoned, and confronted, but when his three-year ministry was over, he had laid the foundation for human redemption. The instrument of his plan is a preacher, preaching well, taking his calling seriously, and speaking in power the whole counsel of God. To fill our office well is to diminish any high-mindedness by laying aside all pomp. We then can preach finely tuned, effective sermons.

Afterword

By this time the difference between a textbook on preaching and a philosophy of preaching has become evident. I did not set out to tell the reader in detail how to craft a sermon. I rather hoped to describe, define, examine, exhibit, portray, and, yes, challenge preachers to biblical preaching. I rather dislike summaries, since I have always had the feeling that anything that can be said in two paragraphs is probably what should have been read in the first place, if only to save time. But wrap-ups do make some sense, and thus I conclude as I began, calling your attention one final time to the outline of our thought.

The Spirit was the primary and yet elusive beginning of this book. We consistently referred to him as the essential but liminal part of our homiletic. Defying homiletical machinations of any sort, the Spirit alone makes the sermon more than a speech. Still, the Spirit never relates primarily to the sermon but rather to the preacher. His empowering work is not passed to preachers beneath the ribbon that wrapped the parchment at seminary graduation. Nor does his authentication of the sermon ever come from merely studying homiletics or from the development of our communication skills. His presence is always and only at the end of our hungering and thirsting after righteousness that we may be filled. Thus the work of the Spirit can best be described as hunger. Without the hunger, we are not God's ambassadors, and the sermon can at best possess only human nobility. It cannot possess the Word of God that in any serious way can become the words of God.

The word, in this philosophy of preaching, came in the second part as Word of God which imparts both authenticity and authority. Authenticity is that quality of the sermon that makes us worth listening to. Authority is that communicative force that makes it impossible not to listen. In understanding all aspects of the Word, we looked at words as the crafting of the sermon. As the Bible-Word combines with the art of the sermon-word, the best possibility for making Christ foundational to all of Christian experience is born.

The story section of this book calls our age to listen because we have learned the use of parable, plot, and image. Even those of us who feel that we may not have gifts in the area of storytelling are under the compulsion to do all we can to become the best of all possible raconteurs. If storytelling as a sermon art is awkward for us at first, we are challenged in this section of the book to see that it is wise and effective to start with tentative beginnings and move as far as we can in the direction of building story intrigue into our sermons.

The final section of this book on preparation and delivery is for me an important and practical way to wind up the volume. Philosophies are not the same as textbooks, but both have the obligation to be practical. The last two chapters of the book, I hope, will serve to make the philosophy seem workable as we use the elements of Spirit, word, and story to make our preaching effective. The organization of our preparation and delivery will keep us from what E. F. Markquart called "sloppy agape,"[1] and our preaching will have escaped from what Paul Harms called "unrelieved dullness."[2]

The great preacher François de Fénelon once counseled that all spiritual work is to "be done in us quietly and peacefully, not as though it could all be accomplished in a single day."[3] Of course, the actual task of becoming a preacher will take a lifetime, but if preaching gets better and develops its art, it will major on these three things: It will be driven by the Spirit, crying, "My speech and my preaching was not with enticing words of man's wisdom but in demonstration of the Spirit and of power" (1 Cor. 2:4 KJV). It will also major on the "exposition of the Word of God contained in the Scriptures in such a way as to bring home its saving and liberating truth to the hearers."[4]

Finally, it will tell stories, never forgetting that "the ear needs an image to help it remember."[5]

This divine trinity of advisors—Spirit, word, and story—will give us a rich, well-deserved influence. Rightly armed with such influence, we shall advance with strong, indicative preaching, committed, imperative preaching, and preaching made rich by parable and image. Ever maturing in the power of delivery, the spirit of our dynamic exhortation will be born again with the dawn of each new Sunday.

Appendix: Outline of the Book

I. Spirit
  A. The Imperative Mystery of Preaching (chapter 1)
    1. Introduction
      a) Sermon or speech?
      b) Here-and-now or otherworldly
      c) The world at hand
    2. The Intrigue of Otherworldliness
      a) The lure of what we don't have
      b) Answering life, not questions
      c) The force of mystery and the pastor's devotional life
      d) Preaching as force rather than form
      e) Guarding spiritual integrity
        (1) Every person has a right to see spiritually
        (2) The right to abandon "things as they are"
    3. The Silent Center
    4. The Compulsion of Mystery
      a) The drawing of the mind
      b) The awakenings of God
      c) Desire and the divine takeover
      d) Surprise and emotion: the double evidence
    5. Conclusion
  B. The Spirit as Teacher (chapter 2)
    1. Introduction
    2. Teaching the Unteachable
    3. Preparing: Our Work and His Work
    4. Preaching True Reality
      a) Three biblical models
      b) Confrontational apologetics
      c) Staying human in the course of speaking for God
    5. The Demand of God

6. God and Ultimate Reckoning
7. Conclusion
C. The Spirit as Counselor (chapter 3)
1. Introduction
   a) The grappling sermon
   b) Keeping company with questions
2. Sermonizing Counsel
   a) Intimacy and emotion
   b) Avoiding emotion for its own sake
   c) The agony and joy of community
   d) Liberating, not solving
   e) The vulnerable shepherd
3. Comforter and Identity
   a) Stroking the "like" need
   b) Undersaved, oversaved
   c) Stretching congregational identity
   d) Congregational identity and the pastor
4. Comfort and Nurture
5. Conclusion
D. The Spirit as Power (chapter 4)
1. Introduction
   a) Preacher and prophet
   b) Two kinds of power
   c) Two New Testament concepts
2. Integrity
   a) Being earnest
   b) Being right
      (1) Big rights, little rights
      (2) The four sources of pulpit power
   c) The power of integrity
      (1) Telling the saving truth
      (2) A good man speaking
      (3) The issues of sermon focus
3. The God View and the Channel of Power
   a) The Book of God
   b) God's concern for human behavior
      (1) Preaching repentance
      (2) Preaching to the now
      (3) Preaching on the right kind of sin
      (4) Preaching on the sins of the church
      (5) Preaching on the negative subject in a positive way
4. Power and the Sermon's Vitality
   a) Inspiration
   b) Information

   c) Variety
   d) Application
  5. Power Is the Waiting Factor
   a) Waiting before we preach
   b) Waiting while we preach
   c) Avoiding the mid-sermon search for the Spirit
   d) Waiting as tenure in ministry
  6. Conclusion
II. Word
 A. The Bible in Preaching (chapter 5)
  1. Introduction
  2. Feeding
   a) The war against biblical illiteracy
   b) Definition, description, prescription
  3. Authority
   a) The erosion of biblical authority
   b) Authority and ego
   c) The sermon must emerge from Scripture
  4. Things Necessary to Salvation
  5. Biblical Relevance
   a) A "right-now" scriptural ethic
   b) The goal of hermeneutics
   c) Overcoming two seductions
  6. Conclusion
   a) Deepening, broadening
   b) Solitude, Scripture, and sermon preparation
 B. The Word as Art (chapter 6)
  1. Introduction
  2. No Time to Waste
   a) Rhetoric versus desperation
   b) Steeped in the library or the purposes of God?
   c) Simplicity and the elements of zeal
  3. The Coming of Art
   a) The rise of the American sermon as art
   b) The theater tendency
  4. How Then Shall We Preach?
   a) The loss of art and discipline
   b) Motivation with creativity
   c) Urgent without "hokey"
  5. The Pitfalls of Urgency
   a) Meandering
   b) Volume
   c) Melodrama
  6. The Pitfalls of Artistry

     a) Flash, not steamy incandescence
     b) No common sense
     c) Avoiding artistic snobbery
  7. Declaring Artistically
     a) Seeing the Bible as it really is
       (1) Reading it well
       (2) The Scripture monologue
       (3) Liturgy and response
       (4) Scripture anthems and choruses
     b) Adding brightness to the sermon
       (1) Paralleling
       (2) Intersecting
       (3) Contrast illustrating
       (4) Illustrating from the arts
  8. Conclusion
C. The Word as Craft (chapter 7)
  1. Introduction
  2. Wordsmithing
     a) Elocution
     b) The serious art of wordsmithing
     c) Economizing word choice
     d) Respecting our art form
     e) Poetry—glorious economy
  3. Words: The Medium of Sermon as Craft
     a) Becoming a master of words
     b) Developing sensuous language
     c) Using the shortest possible synonym
     d) Managing words
     e) Using action language
     f) Balance
  4. *Logos* Word, *Rhema* Word
     a) Distinguishing these two words
     b) Words precedent to points
  5. *Dabar:* The Word That Is More Than Word
     a) Word as event
  6. Sins of Sermons
     a) Too many words
     b) Undermanaging our words
     c) Paying attention to first line, last line
       (1) First line and argument
       (2) First line and the issue of place
       (3) First line and the meeting of persons
       (4) First line and mood
       (5) First line and poetic beginnings

7. Conclusion
D. The Word as Reputation (chapter 8)
  1. Introduction
  2. Mobility
    a) Static versus movement
    b) Enemies of mobility
      (1) Predictability
      (2) Ostentatious style
      (3) The terminology trap
    c) Questions the mobile sermon must answer
      (1) Is this professional?
      (2) Does it move without distraction?
      (3) Does the sermon avoid colloquialisms and clichés?
    d) Being mobile, being human
  3. Authenticity
    a) Personal authenticity
      (1) Preacher as moral model
      (2) How true are his words?
      (3) Does he acknowledge what is borrowed?
      (4) Authenticity—the chief ingredient of lasting motivation
    b) According dignity to all
      (1) Overinfluencing and nagging
      (2) Avoiding depersonalizing pulpit arrogance
    c) Recognizing who we are psychologically
    d) Not wasting the listener's time
    e) Replacing sermonic threat with affirmation
      (1) Does the word scold or exalt personhood?
      (2) Does this sermon thank or take for granted?
      (3) Does this sermon rebuke, or threaten?
  4. Incarnation
    a) Medium and message
  5. Conclusion
III. Story
  A. The Sermon as Story (chapter 9)
    1. Introduction
      a) Preaching: The grand bridge
      b) The foolishness of preaching
    2. His Story
      a) Once upon a time history
      b) Words—the building blocks of image
      c) Literature and history
        (1) Christianity: the literary religion
        (2) Truth and symbol
        (3) The evangelical seduction

3. Our Story
   a) The once-upon-a-time of saving history
   b) The once-upon-a-time of our existentialism
   c) Metaphorizing the story
4. The Storytellers
   a) Story preaching versus precept preaching
   b) The faults of oral-exegesis sermons
      (1) Notebook academics
      (2) Knowing rather than being
      (3) Notebook arrogance
   c) Biblical examples of story preachers
   d) Story, the conqueror
5. Conclusion
   a) Do stories produce change?
   b) Are stories a real product?
   c) Is storytelling a special talent?
B. The Story as Ultimate Truth (chapter 10)
1. Introduction
   a) The rise of the precept-exegesis sermon
   b) The demand for pulpit content
   c) Ultimate precept, ultimate story
   d) Ultimate truth and the variety of story forms
   e) *Teleios,* the short story
   f) Story as human dignity
2. Ultimate Truth Is the Only One That Matters
   a) Pulpit time and story priority
   b) Story volume versus content
   c) Sermon as the hope document
3. Ultimate Truth Is Nonreducible
4. Ultimate Truth Is Common Sense
   a) Reasonable glory—reasonable story
   b) A reasonable saving story
   c) The reasonable mystery
   d) Elemental stories reveal our identity
5. Stories Become the Ultimate Metaphor of Life
   a) Fictions define our world
   b) Stories as death metaphors
6. Conclusion
C. The Story as Relational Truth (chapter 11)
1. Introduction
   a) The story as precept lubrication
   b) The story confession of the church
   c) Skeleton
   d) Pulpit as symbol

A. Notes on Preparation (chapter 13)
1. Introduction
2. Life Preparation
   a) Total person, total world
   b) Testimonial preaching
   c) Insight by polarity
      (1) Experiential/academic
      (2) Observational/existential
   d) Life as university
   e) Scripture as basic
3. Long-Term Preparation
   a) Buying the bank
   b) The annual view
   c) The series view
   d) The spiritual growth of the whole church
4. Short-Term Preparation
5. Gathering the Sermon
   a) Practicing quotes and reviewing memory work
   b) Rehearsing special phraseology
   c) Marking the outline
   d) Extenders and clippers
   e) The altar call
B. Notes on Delivery (chapter 14)
1. Introduction
2. The Psychology of Delivery
   a) Identity
   b) Motivation
   c) Emotion
3. The Integrity of Delivery
   a) "I am what I appear to be"
   b) "I trust you to choose for yourself"
   c) "I respect your dignity and worth"
   d) "I appreciate your attendance at my sermon and this church"
4. The Process of Delivery
   a) Eye-to-eye and heart-to-heart delivery
   b) Rules for good communication
      (1) Balancing personal distractions with professionalism
      (2) Balancing energy and content
      (3) Opening, closing, and titling
      (4) Homily versus oration

Notes

Introduction

1. R. E. C. Browne, cited in Eugene L. Lowry, *Doing Time in the Pulpit* (Nashville: Abingdon Press, 1985), 56.

2. G. K. Chesterton, *Saint Thomas Aquinas* (Garden City, N.Y.: Image Books, 1956), 180.

3. I encourage you to see David Buttrick, *Homiletic* (Philadelphia: Fortress Press, 1987); Donald Coggan, *Preaching: The Sacrament of the Word* (New York: Crossroads, 1988); and Fred B. Craddock, *Preaching* (Nashville: Abingdon Press, 1985).

4. Michael Polanyi, cited in Lowry, *Doing Time in the Pulpit*, 11.

5. Lowry, *Doing Time in the Pulpit*, 15.

Chapter 1: The Imperative Mystery of Preaching

1. William Wordsworth, "The World Is Too Much with Us," in Charles H. Woolbert and Severina E. Nelson, *The Art of Interpretive Speech*, 4th ed. (New York: Appleton-Century-Crofts, 1956), 90.

2. Yogi Berra, cited in Tom Peters, *Thriving on Chaos* (New York: Knopf, 1987), 143.

3. Donald Coggan, *Preaching*, 75.

4. Charles Finney, cited in *America's Great Revivals: A Compilation of Articles* (Minneapolis: Dimension Books, Bethany Fellowship, 1970), 64.

5. Coggan, *Preaching*, 75.

6. John Donne, "Devotions upon Mergent Occasions," in *World Treasury of Religious Quotations*, comp. and ed. Ralph L. Woods (New York: Garland Books, 1966).

7. Thomas Merton, *New Seeds of Contemplation* (New York: New Directions, 1961), 22.

8. Harold Fickett Jr., *The Holy Fool* (Westchester, Ill.: Crossway, 1983), 69.

9. David R. Mains, *The Sense of His Presence* (Waco: Word, 1988), 112.

10. Cited in Elisabeth Elliot, *Discipline: The Glad Surrender* (Grand Rapids: Revell, 1970).

11. T. S. Eliot, "Ash Wednesday," in *The Waste Land and Other Poems* (New York: Harcourt Brace Jovanovich, 1962), 63.

12. Howard Anke, *One Divine Moment*, ed. Robert E. Coleman (Old Tappan, N.J.: Revell, 1970).

13. Jonathan Edwards, cited in Arthur Wallis, *Revival: The Rain from Heaven* (Grand Rapids: Revell, 1979), 49–51.

14. C. G. Finney, *Autobiography of Charles Finney* (Bethany, 1979), cited in Winkie Pratney, comp., *Revival* (Springdale, Pa.: Whitaker House, 1984), 131–32.

15. Earl Palmer, *The 24-Hour Christian* (Downers Grove, Ill.: InterVarsity, 1987), 25.

235

Chapter 2: The Spirit as Teacher

1. Rudyard Kipling, cited in Homer K. Buerlein, *How to Preach More Powerful Sermons* (Philadelphia: Westminster Press, 1986), 59.

2. Cicero, cited in Buerlein, *How to Preach*, 58.

3. Robert Louis Stevenson, cited in Edward F. Markquart, *Quest for Better Preaching* (Minneapolis: Augsburg, 1985), 106.

4. Helmut Thielicke, *The Trouble with the Church* (Grand Rapids: Baker, 1965), 52, cited in Markquart, *Quest for Better Preaching*, 29.

5. Martin Luther, *Deutsche Messe* (1526), cited in Markquart, *Quest for Better Preaching*, 91.

6. John Calvin, *Twenty Centuries of Great Preaching*, 2:38, cited in Pratney, *Revival*, 56.

7. Jonathan Edwards, *Sinners in the Hands of an Angry God*, cited in Pratney, *Revival*, 109.

8. Charles G. Finney, *Revival Lectures* (Grand Rapids: Revell, n.d.), 493, cited in Mains, *The Sense of His Presence*, 69–70.

9. Flannery O'Connor, "Wise Blood," in *Three by Flannery O'Connor* (New York: New American Library, 1983), 72.

10. Jonathan Edwards, *The Life and Diary of David Brainerd*, cited in Pratney, *Revival*, 15.

Chapter 3: The Spirit as Counselor

1. C. S. Lewis, *The Problem of Pain* (New York: Macmillan, 1962), 26.

2. M. Scott Peck, *A Different Drum* (New York: Simon and Schuster, 1987), 106.

3. A. P. Gibbs, *Worship: The Christian's Highest Occupation* (Kansas City: Walterick Publishers, n.d.), 62–64, cited in Mains, *The Sense of His Presence*, 50–52.

4. J. C. Penney, cited in C. Thomas Hilton, "How to Survive Life's Greatest Temptation," *Preaching* (September-October 1987): 14.

5. Charles G. Finney, *Revival Lectures*, 8, cited in Mains, *The Sense of His Presence*, 74.

6. Buttrick, *Homiletic*, 457.

7. Visser't Hooft, cited by Robert E. Webber, *Common Roots* (Grand Rapids: Zondervan, 1978), 163.

8. Gregory the Great, cited in Coggan, *Preaching*, 149.

9. Richard Baxter, *The Reformed Pastor* (Portland: Multnomah, 1982), 93–94.

10. Plato, "Apology," in *The Greek Anthology*, ed. J. W. Mackail (1906), 2:28; cited in Peck, *A Different Drum*, 66.

11. Gary D. Stratman, "To Recognize the Peace of God," *Preaching* (September–October 1987): 27.

12. Norman Cousins, cited in Stratman, "To Recognize the Peace of God," 27.

13. Pascal, cited in Stratman, "To Recognize the Peace of God," 28.

14. J. Wallace Hamilton, cited in Alton H. McEachern, "Communication—God's Problem Too," in *Southern Baptist Preaching Today* (Nashville: Broadman Press, 1987), 247.

15. Martin Marty, "Trusting Faith," in *Practical Christianity*, ed. LaVonne Neff et al. (Wheaton: Tyndale, 1987), 198–99.

Chapter 4: The Spirit as Power

1. Coggan, *Preaching*, 79.

2. Ibid.

3. Charles G. Finney, *Lectures on Revivals of Religion*, cited in Mains, *The Sense of His Presence*, 99.

4. William H. Willimon, "Advent Meditation," *Christian Century* (3 December 1986): 1086.

5. James Daane, *Preaching with Confidence* (Grand Rapids: Eerdmans, 1980), 58 (emphasis added).

6. Charles Spurgeon, cited in Markquart, *Quest for Better Preaching*, 121.

7. Increase Mather, cited in Mains, *The Sense of His Presence*, 167.

8. George Burns, *How to Live to Be 100—or More* (New York: New American Library, 1983), 115.

9. Vernon Grounds, cited in Charles Colson, *Who Speaks for God?* (Westchester, Ill.: Crossway, 1985), 27.

10. James A. Stewart, *Invasion of Wales by the Spirit through Evan Roberts* (Fort Washington, Pa.: Christian Literature Crusade, 1975), 36–37.

11. Woody Allen, cited in Marshall Shelley, "From the Editors," *Leadership* (Summer 1987): 3.

12. Noel Coward, cited in "To Illustrate: Tenacity," *Preaching* 3, no. 1 (July–August 1987): 50.

Chapter 5: The Bible in Preaching

1. Cited in Coggan, *Preaching*, 21, 22.

2. Allan Bloom, *The Closing of the American Mind* (New York: Simon and Schuster, 1987), 60.

3. Leander E. Keck, *The Bible in the Pulpit* (Nashville: Abingdon Press, 1980), 32, 33.

4. Robert Roth, *Story and Reality* (Grand Rapids: Eerdmans, 1973), 38.

5. Keck, *The Bible in the Pulpit*, 120.

6. Elizabeth Achtemeier, cited in Markquart, *Quest for Better Preaching*, 92.

7. Fred W. Meuser, *Luther the Preacher* (Minneapolis: Augsburg, 1983), 35.

8. Charles R. Brown, cited in Markquart, *Quest for Better Preaching*, 105.

9. Bernard L. Manning, *A Layman in the Ministry*, cited in Coggan, *Preaching*, 108.

10. Fred B. Craddock, *As One without Authority* (Nashville: Abingdon Press, 1987), 5.

11. H. Grady Davis, *Design for Preaching* (Philadelphia: Fortress, 1958), 208.

12. David H. C. Read, *Preaching about the Needs of Real People* (Philadelphia: Westminster Press, 1988), 71–72.

Chapter 6: The Word as Art

1. Kate Caffrey, *The Mayflower* (New York: Stein and Day, 1974), 278–79.

2. Herman Melville, *Moby-Dick* (Chicago: William Benton, 1952), 35–36.

3. William E. Hull, "Called to Preach," *Search* (1978): 49.

4. John Ruskin, cited in Hull, "Called to Preach," 53.

5. Mark Twain, *Adventures of Huckleberry Finn* (New York: Norton, 1962), 8.

6. Somerset Maugham, cited in Fred B. Craddock, *Overhearing the Gospel* (Nashville: Abingdon Press, 1978), 17.

Chapter 7: The Word as Craft

1. Buttrick, *Homiletic*, 6.

2. Martin Heidegger, cited in Buttrick, *Homiletic*, 7.

3. Andrew Wyeth, cited in Charles L. Bartow, *The Preaching Moment*, ed. William D. Thompson (Nashville: Abingdon Press, 1981), 94.

4. Emily Dickinson, "A Word," in *Collected Poems of Emily Dickinson* (New York: Avenel Books, 1982), 23.

5. William Stafford, cited in Eugene H. Peterson, *Run with the Horses* (Downers Grove, Ill.: Inter-Varsity, 1983), 30.

6. Peter Marshall, "The Grave in the Garden," in *Mr. Jones, Meet the Master* (Grand Rapids: Revell, 1950), 101, 105.

7. Lewis Carroll, "Through the Looking-Glass," in *The Best of Lewis Carroll* (Secaucus, N.J.: Castle, 1983), 238.

8. Ibid., 233.

9. Alphonsus Liguori, *Love God and Do What You Please!* (Liguori, Mo.: Liguori Publications, 1978), 81.

10. W. E. Sangster, *The Craft of Sermon Construction* (Baskingstoke, England: Pickering & Inglis, 1985), 133–34.

11. Sparhawk Jones, cited in Sangster, *The Craft of Sermon Construction*, 135.

12. Sangster, *The Craft of Sermon Construction*, 124.

Chapter 8: The Word as Reputation

1. Barbara Tuchman, *Practicing History* (New York: Knopf, 1981), 27.

2. Edwin Newman, *Strictly Speaking* (New York: Bobbs-Merrill, 1974), 148.

3. Meuser, *Luther the Preacher*, 47.

4. J. Daniel Baumann, *An Introduction to Contemporary Preaching* (Grand Rapids: Baker, 1972), 149.

5. John Killinger, *Fundamentals of Preaching* (London: SCM Press, 1985), 8.

6. L. Frank Baum, *The Wizard of Oz* (New York: Ballantine Books, 1979), 45.

7. Martin Luther, cited in Meuser, *Luther the Preacher*, 53.

8. Charles Spurgeon, cited in Markquart, *Quest for Better Preaching*, 27.

9. Vance Packard, *The Hidden Persuaders* (New York: David McKay, 1957), 243.

10. Harry Levinson, *The Great Jackass Fallacy* (Cambridge: Harvard University Press, 1973), 10.

11. Jesse S. Nirenberg, *Getting through to People* (Englewood Cliffs, N.J.: Prentice-Hall, 1963), 240.

12. Robert Townsend, *Up the Organization* (Greenwich, Conn.: Fawcett Press, 1973), 70.

13. Ray C. Hackman, *The Motivated Working Adult* (American Management Association, USA, 1969), 22.

14. Levinson, *The Great Jackass Fallacy*, 69.

15. Kenneth Blanchard and Spencer Johnson, *The One-Minute Manager* (New York: William Morrow, 1982), 81.

16. Coggan, *Preaching*, 108.

Chapter 9: The Sermon as Story

1. J. B. Broadbent, cited in Leland Ryken, *Culture in Christian Perspective* (Portland: Multnomah, 1986), 41.

2. Pablo Picasso, cited in Ryken, *Culture in Christian Perspective*, 113.

3. Annie Dillard, *Pilgrim at Tinker Creek*, cited by Philip Yancey, *Open Windows* (Westchester, Ill.: Crossway, 1982), 136–37.

4. T. S. Eliot, cited in Ray C. Stedman, "Preaching in the Future Church," in *Future Church*, comp. Ralph W. Neighbour (Nashville: Broadman Press, 1980), 110.

Chapter 10: The Story as Ultimate Truth

1. John Steinbeck, *The Acts of King Arthur and His Noble Knights* (New York: Farrar, Straus and Giroux, 1976), 313–14.

2. John Hersey, "God's Typhoon," *Atlantic Monthly* (January 1988): 73.

3. Fritz Ridenour, *How to Be a Christian without Being Perfect* (Ventura, Calif.: Regal Books, 1986), 204.

4. William Shakespeare, *Hamlet,* act 3, scene 4, lines 21–23.

5. William Shakespeare, *Romeo and Juliet,* act 5, scene 3, lines 305–6, 309–10.

6. Malcolm Muggeridge, *The Infernal Grove* (New York: Quill, 1973), 68.

7. Walt Whitman, cited in Ruth Miller and Robert A. Greenberg, *Poetry: An Introduction* (New York: St. Martin's Press, 1981), 281.

Chapter 11: The Story as Relational Truth

1. Carl Sandburg, cited in Craddock, *Preaching,* 167–68.

2. Peck, *A Different Drum.*

3. Eugene Peterson, *Working the Angles* (Grand Rapids: Eerdmans, 1987), 19.

4. G. K. Chesterton, "Orthodoxy," in *Basic Chesterton* (Springfield, Ill.: Templegate Publishers, 1984), 7.

5. Donne, "Devotions upon Mergent Occasions," 92.

6. Walt Whitman, cited in Miller and Greenberg, *Poetry: An Introduction,* 9.

7. A. A. Milne, *The House at Pooh Corner* (New York: Dutton, 1961), 147–49.

Chapter 12: The Story as Salvation

1. Ralph L. Lewis with Gregg Lewis, *Inductive Preaching* (Westchester, Ill.: Crossway, 1983), 21.

2. Shakespeare, *Hamlet,* act 2, scene 2, lines 536–37.

3. Herman Melville, *White Jacket,* cited in Peterson, *Working the Angles,* 74.

4. Robert A. Heinlein, *Job: A Comedy of Justice* (New York: Ballantine Books, 1984), 252–53.

5. Ibid., 250.

6. Chesterton, "Orthodoxy," in *Basic Chesterton,* 27.

7. George MacDonald, *The Grand Essentials* (Waco: Word, 1988).

8. Madeleine L'Engle, *Walking on Water,* cited in Ryken, *Culture in Christian Perspective,* 30.

Chapter 13: Notes on Preparation

1. Joseph Sittler, *The Anguish of Preaching* (Philadelphia: Fortress Press, 1966), 12.

2. John Calvin, cited in Buttrick, *Homiletic,* 262.

3. Buerlein, *How to Preach,* 66.

4. Buttrick, *Homiletic,* 308–9.

Chapter 14: Notes on Delivery

1. Ronald J. Allen, *Preaching for Growth* (St. Louis: CBP Press, 1988), 57.

Afterword

1. Markquart, *Quest for Better Preaching,* 99.

2. Paul Harms, *Power from the Pulpit* (St. Louis: Concordia, 1980), 12.

3. François de Fénelon, *Let Go* (Springdale, Pa.: Whitaker House, 1973), 60–61.

4. Coggan, *Preaching,* 112.

5. Markquart, *Quest for Better Preaching,* 196.